FUSTEL DE COULANGES
POLYBIUS AND THE ROMAN
CONQUEST OF GREECE

POLYBIUS AND THE ROMAN CONQUEST OF GREECE
HOW HELLENIC DISUNITY GAVE RISE TO ROMAN RULE

NUMA FUSTEL DE COULANGES

TRANSLATED BY ALFRED NORGAARD

Published in 2023 by Invictus Publishing.

© Matthew Edward Alexander Pedrick. All rights reserved.

No part of this work may be reproduced commercially without the express permission of the publisher.

French title: "Polybe, ou, la Grèce conquise par les Romains"

Cover art: "The Sack of Corinth" by Thomas Allom

ISBN: 9781068416354

CONTENTS

Introduction	4
I. Civil War among the City-States	8
II. The Moderate Men	28
III. The Two Leagues	42
IV. The Two Parties	54
V. The Friends of Liberty	72
VI. Polybius in Rome	104
VII. The Last Struggle of Democracy against Rome	128
Conclusion	144

"How savage the civil war was, and all the more shocking for being the first to take place. For later, virtually the whole Hellenic world suffered this convulsion; everywhere there was internal strife. The democratic leaders called in the Athenians and the aristocrats called in the Lacedæmonians. In peace-time, they would have had neither the excuse nor the will to invite such intervention, but in times of war, when alliances were available to either party to the detriment of their opponents and thereby their own advantage, there were ready opportunities for revolutionaries to call in foreign support...Civil war thus spread among the cities, and those who came to it later took lessons, it seems, from the precedents set, progressing to new and far greater extremes in the ingenuity of their machinations and the atrocity of their reprisals...until even blood became a weaker tie than party."

– Thucydides, *The Peloponnesian War*

INTRODUCTION

Polybius is the last writer of free Greece and a historian of conquest. His writings, however, are inspired neither by regret for the loss of independence, nor by animosity towards the conquerors; rather, he narrates the long history of the subjugation of his country without indignation or pain. He does not exhibit indifference, yet neither does he possess the impartiality of a historian – indeed, he openly sides with the victors. One can sense his contentment, happiness even, in seeing Greece submit.

There is no doubt that he loves his homeland – the honesty and nobility of his character protect him from any suspicion of treason. Let us not confuse him with the likes of Diophanes and Callicrates, whose conduct he vehemently condemns. He served his country, even in Rome, alongside Scipio Æmilianus; he dared to contest the resentment of the conquerors for the memory and statues of Philopoemen; after the capture of Corinth, he refused to enrich himself with the ruin of his compatriots. Whether acting or writing, we see him ever eager for the prosperity of his nation, concerned about its future or otherwise lamenting its faults. While he may not hold it in the highest esteem, he does express a sincere affection; his book exudes a love of Greece, as well as an admiration for Rome.

So how can it be, we may ask, that Polybius displays not a trace of regret for the perishing freedom? That an honest citizen devoted to his country can rejoice in the success of the public enemy, and that this preference is not treason but almost patriotism, is a fact worthy of some attention. Furthermore, if a thorough study of this era shows us that he is indeed no different from his fellow citizens, and that his sentiments reflect those of a large part of his nation, one can hope to find an explanation for the conquest of Greece.

The legions did not do everything; the politics of the Roman Senate did not prepare everything. The Greeks, in truth, were intimately involved in the work of their own subjugation, and it would seem that their sentiments and moral dispositions arguably contributed more than did the strength and skill of their conquerors. We shall attempt to demonstrate here, through Polybius' work and Polybius himself, how the heart of the second century Greek was inclined to be conquered, and how Rome duly conducted its conquests. What in the fortune of Rome should be attributed to the virtues and wisdom of the Romans has been well explained. The intention here is to highlight the part played by the vanquished in the rise of this marvellous fortune and how they themselves contributed to it.

A Roman historian, himself something of a rhetorician, said of Greece that to penetrate it was to master it, "*introisse victoria fuit*".[1] This should not be understood to mean that Greece, without strength and energy, was easy prey for any conquering force that came along. Livy shows us that it was not without trepidation that the Romans undertook wars against Philip, Perseus, and Antiochus. Greece, demonstrably, was not lacking in vigour. It was richer than Italy, and it still had an abundance of manpower. Polybius claims that the Achæan League alone could field thirty or forty thousand soldiers. Greece still possessed the Ætolian cavalry, the Macedonian phalanx, and the fleets of Rhodes; it had the favourable disposition of its land and its mountains that halted any approaching enemy; it had the respect it inspired and the memory of its ancient glory, which, if it did not serve to invigorate it, could at least make its adversaries less bold. This Greek race, in which the military spirit was not yet extinguished, was still capable of measuring itself against Rome. Yet Greece, eternally divided, had not the desire, it seems, to do what was within its means.

---

1. Lucius Annæus Florus, *Epitome Rerum Romanorum*, 1.23.7.11

I

ARISTOCRACY AND DEMOCRACY IN GREECE
CIVIL WAR AMONG THE CITY-STATES

Ancient Greek society was constituted through the municipal system, and as such, the new spirit of freedom it brought into the world did not initially lend itself to the establishment of large societies. If one rejected the despotism of the East, it was also necessary to abandon the grand and persistent unity of Eastern societies. Fragmentation thus prevailed in this land where nature itself, long before humans, had already delineated so many divisions, and where the mountains and the sea had carved it so extensively. Each concentration of people formed a state; each city was sovereign. Some religious institutions did remind the cities of their brotherhood, but never to the extent that their independence was diminished.

The municipal spirit was so powerful among the Greek people that it dominated the genius of all its statesmen. Greece had admirable legislators, and modern thinkers have added nothing to their science of balancing powers and ensuring the harmony of the diverse elements of a state. Their legislation, however, was only intended for a city and would have been powerless to govern an entire nation. Even the philosophers themselves – who had ample opportunity to create an ideal republic – limited human association within the confines of city walls. Plato, whose imagination was burdened by the task of governing a large number of people, allowed only 5,000 citizens in his ideal republic.

As a consequence, the patriotism of the Greeks hardly extended beyond the limits of the city. Since few individuals had a clear conception of a common homeland, few also felt attached to it and devoted themselves to it. All affections and energies were given to the polis. During the Persian War, Sparta would have willingly sacrificed all of Greece to defend only the Peloponnese. Herodotus does not criticise those Ionians who, at Salamis, fought more fiercely against the Greeks than the Persians themselves; nor was Thucydides especially harsh on the Spartans and Athenians who sent ambassadors to the Great King. Aristophanes portrayed Athens' policy on stage without condemning it.[1] The political mindset of the Greeks seldom rose above the idea of the city. Corinth did not understand why it had anything in common with Megara, or Argos with Sparta, or Megalopolis with Mantinea. Between two neighbouring cities, it often seemed that only animosity could exist.

One of the consequences of this extreme division was an uninterrupted series of bloody wars – wars that never fostered unity. If a city had been conquered, it had to be destroyed or enslaved, for the vanquished were not integrated into the victorious state and had no share in the city. The Greeks only realised much later that a state could be composed of two cities enjoying equal rights, with both participating in the common government. While they were very skilled at legislating for a city, in the event that they expanded their power, they lacked the requisite science of governance, resulting in the enslavement of cities due to the inability to administer them properly. Since no city had been strong enough to impose absolute rule on Greece, Greece was never able to be united.

When threatened by powerful empires, Greece had indeed managed to form several confederations. These attempts, however – made in response to immediate danger – endured no longer than the threat itself. Soon, only those who had an interest in transforming the confederation into an empire remained committed

---

1. Aristophanes, *Acharnians*

to the alliance. The other cities, which had at one point eagerly formed the confederation, were even more eager to break it, claiming that their freedom was at risk. The spirit of municipal independence rapidly destroyed that which danger and momentary prudence had produced. Greece, always wavering between the need for a central power and the love of autonomy, had never been able to establish either one, or secure the other, constantly oscillating between fragmentation and subjugation.

The example of Greece would readily lead one to believe that no political regime presents more challenges than the municipal system, and that governing a city is more difficult than governing a nation. On a narrower stage, passions are more intense, enmities more personal, and enemies ever present. It requires a people to be doubly wise so as not to be poorly governed.

In almost every Greek city, there were two classes: the rich and the poor. During the time of Polybius, the aristocracy that was once closely associated with traditional religious functions had disappeared, and there was no longer any distinction of birth. Only wealth established class within the city.

Wealth, which can foster endeavours both private and public, further learning, and even patronise the arts, greatly contributing to the splendour of a civilisation, can also give rise to corruption and civil strife, as it did among the Greeks. In our society,[1] thanks to a rapid and generally fair circulation, wealth passes from the rich to the poor and from the poor to the rich to a greater extent, flowing from hand to hand and leaving some degree of prosperity everywhere. In Greece, however, slavery made it considerably less accessible to the lower class, and shame was attached in almost every city to labour, the respectable aspiration of that very class. One had to already be rich to become richer – money was stagnant. The rich did not know, or care, how to make it flow through society because they were unaware of, or merely indifferent to, the expenses imposed upon the wealthy by luxury, art, and custom. The poor did not know how to attract it to themselves because their indolence equalled their frugality. It was only through taxation that the state could alleviate this inequality and establish some circulation of money. As a result, taxes weighed heavily on the rich: they were required to fund trierarchies and choregi;[2] their magistracies were costly. On the other hand, the triobol was distributed at assemblies and the theatre to bring money down to the idle masses. Confiscation was sometimes necessary. These unjust and ineffective means sometimes impoverished the rich, but they could not enrich the poor. Inequality continued to grow as only the rich could acquire meaningful wealth,

---

1. France in the middle of the 19ᵗʰ century
2. Pseudo-Xenophon, *Constitution of the Athenians*, 1.13

and fortunes tended to concentrate indefinitely. In Sparta, from the moment donations and purchases were allowed, it took only seven generations for the number of landowners to decrease from nine thousand to one hundred.

Let us imagine, therefore, two classes or two societies in each Greek city: one that possesses and grows richer every day, proud of its easy wealth and eager to preserve it; the other, both needy and indolent, jealous as well as miserable, coveting wealth but lacking the knowledge and means to attain it. These two classes of people became two factions the moment the poor realised that a revolution could make them wealthy, and from that day forward, it needed only for the poor to recognise their numerical advantage for this revolution to become inevitable.

Whenever we witness discord within a city, the rich are always on one side and the poor on the other. The poor wish to acquire wealth, while the rich seek to preserve or regain it. In every civil war, as Polybius teaches us, the goal was to seize the property of the other, "ἵνα διάλλωνται τὰς ἀλλήλων οὐσίας".[1] Every demagogue acted as Molpagoras of Cios did, handing over those who lived comfortably, "τούς ευξαιπουντας τοῖς βιοις",[2] massacring some, exiling others, and distributing their belongings to the people, "τὰς τούτων οὐσίας δημεύων, καὶ διαδιδοὺς τοῖς τοδλοις".[3]

---

1. Polybius, XV, 21; "so that the wealth of each is altered"
2. "those with well-governed lives"
3. "seizing their possessions and distributing them to the needy"

The same historian cites the example of Messene, where the victorious democratic party exiled the rich and distributed their belongings through lotteries.[1] Often, a revolt would be followed by a redistribution of land, while sometimes an abolition of debt was enough. Yet one way or another, either of these two outcomes was demanded by the democracy. Livy warns us that if the Ætolians were in discord, it was because of the great number of debts.[2] He shows us a Roman ambassador who, called as an arbitrator in Thessaly, could only pacify the troubles by reducing the interest on money and establishing annuities for the repayment of capital. Though even this did not prevent the Ætolians from abolishing their debts shortly thereafter, nor the Thessalians from following their example, and both groups plunged into the various disorders of anarchy.

In order for Greece to be united and at peace, it would have been necessary to exclude both opulence and poverty, these two diseases of cities. Sparta, for instance, managed to escape civil strife for so long precisely because it had neither a class of excessively rich or poor citizens. Polybius is right in pointing out that Lycurgus, by banishing greed, had banished discord.[3] Accordingly, when money was introduced into Sparta by Lysander, and especially when the acquisition of wealth became permissible,[4] two

---

1. Polybius, VII, 10   2. Livy, XLII, 5   3. Polybius, VI, 46
4. Plutarch, *Life of Agis*

factions immediately arose, and they displayed as much bitterness as seen in other cities.

Thus, the revolutions in ancient Greece were not simply political, but social. They not only shifted power but wealth as well. The terms democracy and aristocracy, it should be noted, did not have exactly the same meaning then as they do in our time. The constitutions of Greek cities during Polybius' era were quite similar, and in almost all of them, those with citizenship shared political rights equally. Therefore, what we understand as a democratic regime existed almost everywhere. In cases, however, where a small class possessed wealth and wielded great influence, the government was considered aristocratic. In situations where debt abolition, land redistribution, or at least forced loans had recently taken place, the constitution was regarded as democratic. The stronger of the two factions did not limit themselves to political power, and each coup was marked by either confiscation of wealth or forced restitution.

One of the early actions in the life of Aratus, which was noted by ancient writers as uncommon, was the revolution he brought about in Sicyon. This revolution, which resulted in the liberation of many exiles who had been deprived of their property in a previous revolution fifty years prior, required returning their possessions to them and ruining those who had possessed these lands for half a century. Aratus accomplished this, an act which Cicero, who recounts the event, does not find extraordinary but instead rather common. What distinguished Aratus, then, was his ability to find a way, through the generosity of a Ptolemy, to compensate those from whom he took away their property. It is this latter aspect that Cicero admires, while the former was a regular occurrence.[1]

In the Greek context, the words "tyranny" and "freedom" did not possess the same meaning as they do in our contemporary understanding. Under these terms, it was often still the conflict between wealth and poverty that was at play. Tyranny was simply a form of democracy, and this is what distinguished it from the ancient heroic monarchy. As Aristotle said, "while monarchy is established to defend the interests of the elite against the masses, the tyrant's mission is to protect the people against the wealthy. The tyrant always begins as a demagogue, and it is inherent in tyranny to combat the aristocracy".[2] It is likely due to Philip having abandoned the interests of the Greek aristocracy to gain popularity that Polybius suggests he became a tyrant instead of the king he had once been. Again, Cleomenes, who abolished debts and redistributed land, turned the Spartan monarchy into tyranny, according to Polybius.[3] Nicocles, the tyrant

---

1. Cicero, *De Officiis*, II, 23   2. Aristotle, *Politics*, V, 8
3. Polybius, IV, 77

of Sicyon, was the leader of a democracy and had dispossessed the wealthy. As we have seen, one of Aratus' first acts was to restore the property of the wealthy citizens whom the tyrant had exiled. Nabis, too, was nothing more than the leader of the poor against the rich. He laid the foundation of his tyranny by exiling those who held wealth or high birth.[1] As the master of Argos, his first order of business was to confiscate the property of the aristocracy, abolish debts, and redistribute land.[2] The same policy was implemented in Sparta, where he granted fields to the poor and freedom to the slaves.[3] In his war against Achæa and Flamininus, he found ten thousand Lacedæmonians willing to take up arms for him due to his popularity. To ensure his resistance, however, he had to massacre the eighty wealthiest citizens of Sparta.[4]

This is what inequality of fortunes produced among the Greeks; here we can see clearly the absence of political and social foresight among an otherwise exceptional people. Each of these almost daily revolutions should have roused them to work towards preventing their recurrence, avoiding such strife by ensuring a more equitable distribution of wealth or providing better conditions for the poor, by mitigating and managing inequality. Everyone should have sought the solution to this problem: the poor in order

---

1. Polybius, II, 47   2. Polybius, XIII, 6; Livy, XXXII, 38-40
3. Polybius, XI, 12   4. Livy, XXXIV; Diodorus, XXVII, 1

to attain prosperity, the rich to preserve it, and the virtuous citizens to ensure the stability of the state. This is what the Greeks least considered. Aristotle wrote a treatise on economic science, yet even he overlooked this most important aspect. As a result, the aftermath of every revolution resembled one another: the rich were exiled, at the very least, and their property was divided among the most cunning individuals within the populace. Wealth merely changed hands, and the same inequality persisted among fortunes, if not yet more unjustly. This necessitated another revolution, a social condition which forced both the people and the aristocracy to conspire against their homeland in turn. This endured from the Persian Wars until the conquest of Greece by the Romans.

What could become of patriotism in such circumstances? Patriotism, which should not be confused with love for one's native soil, is not, like the latter, an instinctive feeling, invincible, imposed by external nature on all generations inhabiting the same land. Patriotism, by contrast, is a more voluntary and changeable sentiment, subject to various conditions. One loves their country, that is to say, their city or nation, if they love its laws, if they love its leaders, if they are attached to its customs. They love it for the education they have received from it, for the noble examples they find within it, for the virtues it teaches. Ultimately, they love it on the condition that they are convinced that they owe their happiness and the peace they enjoy to it; that they cannot do without it; that it is superior to every other city; that its laws are more just, its decisions more righteous, its glory more resplendent. Patriotism, then, is a blend of gratitude, respect, trust, and pride. But if these sentiments should fade among the citizens due to the mistakes or misfortunes of the rulers, the vices of institutions, or civil war, one will toil in vain to rekindle patriotism.

In the Greek cities beset by disorder, could one truly love laws that were constantly subject to revolutions, always new and ready to perish, almost always the product of violence, and where one party was always a victim? The poor accused the laws of their misery, while the rich resented the confiscations that befell them. The two halves of the population were alternately persecuted and persecutors, and a fellow citizen was an enemy whose wealth one coveted or whose insurrection one feared. Exile, which the Greek republics treated as a game without foreseeing its disastrous consequences, first taught people to live without their homeland and later to fight against it. Proscriptions, civil wars, and armed re-entry into cities gradually led people to regard the polis as an enemy. The initial transient hatred turned into habitual indifference. Each person loved their homeland only as long as their faction reigned, or rather, the homeland was forgotten, and all thoughts, desires, and energies were directed toward the faction. The state became powerless and no longer found devotion or submission in its members. Over time, people lost the sense of duty toward their homeland. They forgot that they ought to respect its laws and judgements, and thus insurrection appeared to be a legitimate right.

The citizen ceased to belong to the city; they left to serve foreigners and shed the blood that they owed to their homeland for anyone willing to pay. Without mentioning Clearchus and his 13,000 soldiers, Iphicrates and Agesilaus in Egypt, or Memnon and his 50,000 Greeks, we see that during Polybius' time, even the Achæans themselves served under the Egyptians and the Carthaginians. Philopoemen, at a time when his homeland was engaged in war, commanded mercenaries in Crete;[1] Lycortas and Polybius would have gone to fight in Egypt during the war of Perseus if the league had allowed them to do so.[2]

The latter-day Greek, avaricious and lacking respect for the state, did not hesitate to enrich himself at its expense. He lived off the public treasury, which is to say, the governed relied on *theoricum* and *triobol*, while the rulers relied on embezzlement, intrigue, and venality. There were cities where the magistrate in

---

1. Plutarch, *Philopoemen & Flamininus; Life of Philopoemen*
2. Polybius, XXIX, 10

charge of the public treasury had to be changed every month, and others every day. "Do not entrust a Greek with the management of a *talent*", says Polybius, "without requiring ten guarantees, ten oaths, and twenty witnesses; and even then, he will deceive you".[1]

All foreigners knew that the Greeks were for sale, either individually and secretly, or openly and by whole cities. Eumenes dared to offer a pension to the Achæan Senate, which refused, it is true, but accepted the interested gifts from Ptolemy.[2] Seleucus, on the verge of conquering Egypt, took care to distribute a hundred talents among the Greeks, and Polybius said of Perseus that, if he had wished, he could have bought Greece.[3]

Finally, the Greeks, no longer bound by any love for their city, saw no reason not to seek the alliance and support of foreigners. Everyone handed Greece over to them and asked in return only for the triumph of their particular faction.

Patriotism is a fertile source of private virtues: it creates great men at the top of the ladder and honest people at the bottom. The habit of submission to the law instils rectitude in souls, while national pride strengthens and elevates character. When one fears committing ill in the city, one is also hesitant to do so in the household. Respect for the state is always an effective deterrent to wrongdoing and a powerful

---

1. Polybius, VI, 56   2. ibid. XXVII, 56; Diodorus, XXIX, 17
3. Polybius, XXVIII, 9

incentive for doing good. Human nature, left to itself, is weak, self-interested, ignorant, and prone to vice. It is incumbent upon each to help one another, to unite and stand together to defend ourselves against so many failings and faults. Each person feels their own powerlessness and seeks advice or support outside of themselves; they turn to religion, law, custom, and the opinions of others. Religion had little authority over the souls of Polybius' Greeks; it did not have the oversight of ethics, the deposit of morality, and the dominion over conscience. The priest, being merely the minister of worship and appearing only in ceremonies, exerted scant influence over the actions of private life. They lacked the sense of honour which is born from the distinction of classes and arises in the highest classes, from the view they held of their own dignity and duties, gradually spreading to the rest of society. This sentiment, which is a combination of pride and selflessness, this self-respect that commands sacrifice, this submission to certain agreed-upon laws that may mislead us but more often serve as a good guide, this honour that is not virtue but makes virtue easier and doubles our strength, is scarcely seen among the Greeks, not, at least, by the time of the Roman conquest. They no longer had the pride of birth which often leads to good actions as they no longer had great families. What remained, insofar as it did, was the respect for and devotion to the city as the last counsellor and last support.

One can imagine the void that must have been created in the Greek soul by the loss of patriotism. Respect for the domestic hearth and love for the family would have largely perished along with it. Those who in public life sought only the satisfaction of their own interests, could they have had any other rule in their private life? What virtues could be inspired by coveted wealth or ill-gotten riches? What sense of justice could endure in the relationships among citizens accustomed to civil wars, in countries where the courts were closed for twenty consecutive years,[1] and where the city, preoccupied with factional struggles, did not have time to establish justice among individuals? "The entire population", says Polybius, "was given over to pride, avarice, and laziness". The same historian points out yet another symptom of corruption: people no longer wanted to marry or care for children born outside of wedlock.[2] Thus, to escape the difficulties and toil of life, they sought refuge in celibacy; they forgot about the family just as they had forgotten about the homeland.

The habit of civil war, by destroying peace, ease, security, and trust, always weakens the idea of reciprocal duties in every heart and extinguishes any sense of humanity. This is especially true when,

---

1. Polybius, XX, 6   2. ibid. XXXVIII, 4

instead of fighting for principles that would at least elevate the soul, people merely quarrel over wealth. When minds and hearts have no other nourishment than such struggles, when political passions fuelled by greed develop in the soul without finding anything to divert them, social relations will soon be distorted, private life will become embittered, all sentiments will be distorted, and a generation of people will be formed who live only to hate, fight, and slaughter each other in turn. According to Aristotle, aristocrats, or in this instance we may say oligarchs, took the following oath: "I swear to be the enemy of the people and to make neither peace nor truce with them".[1] Rarely does the victor content himself with the exile of the vanquished; he massacres him, sometimes out of vengeance and sometimes as a precautionary measure. One can apply to almost all late Greek states what Polybius said about an Arcadian city, "where there was nothing but reciprocal murders, proscriptions, and pillaging".[2] In this state of mind, clemency was always punished, and trust was a mistake. Polybius, for instance, reproaches Archidamus for having trusted Cleomenes.[3] In Cinetha, Arcadia, the Achæan and aristocratic faction, after much strife, finally prevailed, only to succumb to pity and subsequently reopen the city gates to the exiles from the opposing party. True, they made them swear upon the sacred altars of the

---

1. Aristotle, *Politics*, V, 9   2. Polybius, IV, 17   3. ibid. VIII, 1

gods – and with the most solemn oaths that could be demanded of men – to not disturb the established order. "Truly", adds Polybius, "it was at the very moment when, with their hands on the victim's flank, they pronounced these oaths that they were plotting the ruin of their homeland". Indeed, it took only a few days for them to hand the city over to the Ætolians.[1]

Each party was guilty of its own crimes: the aristocracy in Thebes assassinated Brachyllas, the leader of the opposition party; in Messene, they slaughtered Philopoemen. That same city, a year earlier, had seen its two hundred wealthiest citizens massacred by the democrats. Aristomachus in Argos and Nabis in Sparta proscribed or assassinated the wealthy. Philip was suspected of poisoning Aratus.[2] In Athens, the violence of the factions had subsided out of weariness; it was at this time that Sparta began to experience such troubles and conflicts. In a single year, at the beginning of the Social War, Sparta saw its ephors slaughtered twice, the second time on the very altar of Athena. It is worth noting this particular phenomenon among the Greeks, though it is by no means unique to them: neither religion, nor blood ties, nor friendship meant anything to the politically enthralled when compared to the interests of the party. Dion is assassinated by a friend; Timoleon kills his own brother.

---

1. Polybius, IV, 17-18
2. ibid. VII, 10, 14; Livy, XXXII, 14; Plutarch, *Life of Aratus*, 55

Even in the time of Thucydides and the Peloponnesian War, the meaning of words had already begun to change: "to dare everything was considered zealous; a violent man was deemed reliable. It was praiseworthy to retaliate for harm received, even better to be the first to commit harm. Audacity permitted any excess". Thus, civil wars have altered all ideas and principles of reason; they have changed customs and even language; they have overturned the human heart.

Polybius goes even further: he informs us that the cultivation of the land, the courts, the care of sacrifices, the religious festivals and ceremonies were all neglected amid these wars, and there were times when all of this was forgotten.[1] This is because the Greeks have been living in civil war for over ten generations; it has become the habitual, regular, and normal state of the race. They are born into it, live in it, and will die in it. There is almost no aspect of life for individuals or cities that is not connected to this struggle between factions.

---

1. Polybius, V, 106

II

THE MODERATE MEN
PHILOPOEMEN AND POLYBIUS

Amidst these deplorable struggles and crimes, it was still inevitable that a cultured and intelligent race like the Greeks would produce at least a few wise men. Let us study these men in turn. If they are not entirely free from the spirit of faction, we can at least suppose that they are not completely dominated by it. Let us see, through them, to what extent wisdom could protect itself from these passions, what it could save of the human soul, and what it sacrificed for them. Only then can we determine whether it was a sufficient remedy for the country's woes.

When Polybius was born, Achæa was almost the sole place in Greece where moderation was still possible. The habit of civil war had been absent in Achæa for a long time, wherefore such passions were less intense there. No one had personal vendettas to carry out, or to fear, and the characters were thus calmer, and the public spirit wiser. Achæa, like the rest of Greece, had its rich and poor, but the poor had not yet organized themselves into factions and had not compelled the rich to do the same. The cities were generally small, lacking industry and were almost devoid of commerce. The wealth derived from agriculture is the kind which the poor grant the highest and most enduring respect, and it was well enough distributed to not present a striking contrast between opulence and poverty. The rich were less domineering, the poor less greedy than elsewhere, and the crimes of revolution had not as yet made them irreconcilable.

The government of Achæa was therefore guided by a certain spirit of wisdom that was scarcely seen among other Greeks. The aristocracy enjoyed the power that wealth and intellect bestow, but they knew how to handle it. They energetically fought against the people externally but flattered them internally; the government was democratic in its institutions but aristocratic in spirit. "Nowhere else", says Polybius, "will you find more equality, freedom, or true democracy". Indeed, all citizens enjoyed equal rights, and all could participate in the general assemblies of the league indiscriminately. That being said, the political and social state of a Greek city should not be judged solely based on its written constitution. The equality and freedom proclaimed by the law were sometimes tempered and sometimes pushed to excess, depending on customs, public sentiment, and the influence of either class. The letter of the constitution was nearly the same everywhere, but under the same laws, aristocracy and democracy could take turns in ruling. Therefore, other indicators besides the constitution are needed to distinguish which party holds power. Nowhere in Greece at that time did the aristocracy dominate by virtue of written and acknowledged rights. If it could reign, it was through surprise, cunning, and, above all, by keeping the common people ignorant of its rule.

Thus, among the Achæans, the law is for the people, but the power lies with the aristocracy. The law grants the people the election of the strategos,[1] but since this magistracy is costly,[2] it is necessary for the strategos to be chosen from the wealthy class. In Achæa, young men from prominent families form the cavalry corps. Plutarch highlights the authority and power of this corps, which holds the honours, and Polybius tells us that all those who aspired to become strategos took great care to flatter them.[3]

The people had as many rights as they could demand. All powers emanated from the general assembly, to which all citizens were admitted. It

---

1. Polybius, IV, 14; XXVI, 3; XL, 1   2. ibid. XXVIII, 7
3. Polybius, X, 22; Plutarch, *Life of Philopoemen*, 7, 18; Livy, XXXIX, 49

appointed magistrates, decided on peace and war, and even judged strategoi when necessary. We see Aratus defending himself before the people after an unsuccessful expedition. Nevertheless, aristocratic cunning had protected against the dangerous power of this assembly. Entry was only allowed at the age of thirty, which already served as a guarantee, as the most restless individuals were excluded. Moreover, to attend, one had to leave their city and work, and few men had the inclination or ability to do so. Polybius warns us that the lower-class people abstained from attending the assemblies for a long time. The general meeting only took place once a year at a fixed time. Outside of that, the people could only be summoned by a decree of the magistrates, and then only for a specific and previously indicated subject. Such formalities caused delays and difficulties; there was clear reluctance to summon the people. Furthermore, we only see questions of peace, war, and alliances submitted to their decisions; everything related to internal politics is carefully kept away from the people's eyes. In the absence of the assembly and without waiting for its orders, a senate composed of delegates from the cities would judge and handle all affairs. The strategos, appointed for one year, is actually only the president of the senate and the leader of the army; the true power does not belong to him or the people but to the senate. All of this forms a mixture of democracy and aristocracy, wherein the latter dominates but without excess and violence.

This spirit of prudent aristocracy is especially evident in the Arcadian city of Megalopolis. It was founded in the year following the Battle of Leuctra and was the last city to be established among the Greek states. It had no history of discord or animosity. Its people were wise; there were no factions among them. Throughout the two centuries of its independence, Megalopolis consistently followed the same path: the aristocracy there was always moderate, and democracy never took hold. The spirit of Epaminondas lived among this people; it was the inspiration behind Philopoemen.[1]

The city of Megalopolis never wavered in its distaste for the popular party. Like the entire aristocracy of Greece, it declared its support for Philip, the father of Alexander.[2] When later Polysperchon, in his struggle against Cassander, incited the democratic parties in each of the cities, and at his instigation the enraged multitude in every city massacred or exiled the wealthy, Megalopolis alone remained free from such turmoil and violence, remaining loyal to the aristocracy and the friendship of Cassander. Polysperchon besieged the city with all his forces, but found not a single supporter within its

---

1. Plutarch, *Life of Philopoemen*, 3
2. Polybius, IX, 28; XVII, 14; Pausanias, VIII, 13

walls, and was forced to retreat in the face of the unity and determination of its citizens.[1] Megalopolis relentlessly fought against democracy, enduring sieges by Agis, being overthrown and burned by Cleomenes, all without ever accepting peace with the tyrants. It was the first to call Antigonus Doson into the Peloponnese, and its soldiers contributed to his victory at Sellasia. Polybius bestowed upon it the rare praise that Cleomenes had no friend there and could not find a traitor. It was not the same in other cities, even within the league. Cleomenes had his supporters in Argos, in Troezen, in Epidaurus, in Corinth, and even in Sicyon, within the sight of Aratus. It was always the democratic faction to which he offered hope that all debt would be abolished.[2]

Megalopolis, founded by Epaminondas to be the capital of Arcadia, became the most important city of the Achæan Confederation. After Aratus, almost all the men who led the league were born in Megalopolis. It was the consistency of its policies, more than its material strength, that led to this city taking the leadership of the confederation. As long as it held that position, which lasted until around the time of the war against Perseus, it instilled an aristocratic policy in Achæa.

Philopoemen was from Megalopolis, and by birth he belonged to the aristocracy. He had two

---

1. Diodorus, XVIII, 68   2. Plutarch, *Life of Cleomenes*

philosophers from the Academy as his teachers, but they seemed to be less concerned with teaching him speculative theories and more focused on imparting the principles of aristocratic governance. These two men, Ecdemus and Demophanes, had fled from tyrannical rule, lived in exile, and returned to their homeland only to overthrow it. These same men joined forces with Aratus to drive out Nicocles from Sicyon. They were the first mentors of Philopoemen.[1]

Polybius was himself a student of Philopoemen and the son of Lycortas. These three men almost form a single character, so unified is their politics amidst very diverse circumstances. They are the wise men of Greece, belonging to the small number of individuals who are not completely dominated by personal interest or enmity, and who dedicate the best part of their thoughts to the pursuit of the public good. Polybius rises above the miserable interests that divide his fellow citizens. At a time when most Greeks were thinking only of gaining or retaining wealth in each of their revolutions, he reminds them that the true science of government has a different purpose, "to instil virtue and wisdom into private life, and to promote moderation and justice in public life".[2]

Polybius was deeply struck by the troubles of Greece; it is evident in his book that he sought some form of remedy. He studied the factions that tear cities

---

1. Polybius, X, 22; Plutarch, *Life of Philopoemen*, 1   2. Polybius, VI, 47

apart, and observed the excesses and vices of each. The rich are ambitious, the poor are turbulent and covetous. If the various forms of government are just and moderate in their origins, abuse soon creeps in. Monarchy quickly turns into tyranny, aristocracy degenerates into violent oligarchy, democracy becomes corrupt, and the masses become stronger than the law. From then on, each of these regimes is powerless to govern society because the excesses generate too much animosity, leading to punishment and revenge. The monarchy is overthrown by the nobles, the aristocracy is struck down by the people, and democracy gives birth to a tyrant. The cycle of revolutions continues endlessly because each of these governments has been taken to extremes. These abuses are inherent in each of them, "like rust to iron; like worms to wood". No one can escape them; each has within itself its own vice and, at the same time, its germ of destruction. Thus, in Polybius' view, all parties are equally condemnable; they are all tainted by an original disease. The civil wars, the series of revolutions, and the misfortunes of Greece are attributable to their excesses. The remedy, therefore, did not lie in the triumph of any one of them; neither monarchy, nor aristocracy, nor democracy could save Greece.

Yet Polybius, as an impartial judge, sees also the merits of each of these forms of government.

Monarchy appears to him as just and good, provided that it is founded more on reason than on force. He appreciates aristocracy, the government of the best, as long as power is combined with virtue and wisdom. Equality also seems to him a precious good, and the will of the majority is for him the true source of all legitimate power; thus, he also appreciates democracy, at least if the people "have maintained the habit of worshipping the gods, respecting the elders, and obeying the laws".

The idea that there is something good in all three of these forms of government led Polybius, like some wise thinkers of other times, to believe that the best political system would be one that combines all three. It seems desirable to take from each of them their qualities while avoiding their weaknesses. Let monarchy, aristocracy, and democracy associate and merge in the city. Isolated, each of these governments has caused countless troubles for Greece; so let us try to unite them instead. There is no need to bring the axe down on Greek society, to violently eliminate an entire party, assuming that such a thing is even possible. On the contrary, what Polybius desires is for all parties to come together to contribute to the governance of the state; he does not want the city to miss out on the strengths of any of them, and for all to be able to contribute to its prosperity. The government he envisions for Greece is one where all factions are united, that is to say, where there are no longer any factions.

Indeed, there were still a few wise men in Greece who had not entirely surrendered to political passions, who detested excess and understood the cost of conflict. They did not wish to belong to either of the two extreme parties and therefore strove to maintain a middle ground between these two bitter enemies, between those who vied, interminably it seems, for control of the cities.

Alas, the wisdom of a few men cannot compensate for the wisdom lacking in a nation. Polybius wishes to merge all parties within the state, but he does not seem to realise that by introducing monarchy, aristocracy, and democracy simultaneously, he would also invite many different interests and feuds. These well-ordered systems devised by thoughtful individuals are too intricate, and their mechanisms too delicate for the hands of the people; they shatter them upon being touched.

Polybius is, of course, not entirely impartial. While he despises both factions, his animosity is likely stronger towards the popular party. Due to his birth and upbringing, he belongs to the aristocracy, though he is wary of its excesses. By setting limits, he aims to save it from its greatest enemy: abuse.

He distinguishes himself from most of his fellow citizens only in being more moderate than them. Yet would he be able to instil this moderation in Greek society? Would he even be able to maintain it within himself? When confronted with democracy and its demands, from the peaceful heights where he contemplates constitutions as a philosopher, he suddenly finds himself thrust into the fray, where moderation is no longer possible. Because he is human, he is compelled to take a side, to make a decisive choice and fight. This is precisely the story of his life. He had always sought to distance himself from factions, desiring to remain neutral in the struggle between aristocracy and democracy. Circumstances, however, would not allow for such impartiality, and at the decisive moment, he had no choice but to act precisely as if he did belong to one faction.

Even in his writings, he is not wholly without contradiction – a person cannot ever be steered purely by wisdom and reason. When Polybius engages in dissertations, he does so as a philosopher; when he acts or recounts events, however, the man of action and the historian do not always possess the same disinterestedness and moderation. Despite his principles, he too experiences hatred and affection. He deeply detests the popular party, which he refers to as "the party of troublemakers". He seizes every opportunity to belittle the cities where it holds sway, and his hatred for tyrants bursts forth on every page. "Does the name of a tyrant not imply the greatest iniquity? Does it not encompass all the crimes of which human nature is capable?" he asks.[1] "The murder of a tyrant", he says elsewhere, "is a source of glory".[2] While he acknowledges that Hiero acquired power in Syracuse without massacring or exiling any citizens, he simply remarks that "of all that one can witness, this is truly the most astonishing thing".[3] Nabis, meanwhile, is regarded by him as a monster whose every action has been a crime.

Philip, by contrast, is seen to be a good king so long as he adheres to Aratus' aristocratic policy; should he abandon it, he becomes a detestable tyrant who embodies nothing but vice, greed, and sacrilege.[4]

It is only too easy for a person to deceive themselves. They believe they are wise, yet they are driven, ultimately, by passion; they claim impartiality in one moment of reflection, only to reveal their preferences and biases in the next. What individual is strong enough, with their own intellect alone, to resist the powerful and incessant influence of deeply ingrained ideas? It is rare and difficult to be true to oneself; one adopts thoughts and sentiments as the language of other men. Polybius was born Greek and as such he is inescapably attached to a faction. Despite

---

1. Polybius, II, 59   2. ibid, II, 56   3. ibid, VII, 8   4. ibid, V, 77

being among the more moderate within his party, he nevertheless remains a member of the aristocratic faction. Thus, even the wise themselves are dominated by the perpetual conflicts that fill the life of cities; they are unable to escape factions, let alone eradicate them from Greece and restore peace to their country.

III

THE TWO LEAGUES
THE ARISTOCRATIC LEAGUE AND THE DEMOCRATIC LEAGUE

The quarrelling between parties thus dominated public life; these passions and enmities were masters of the soul. We have seen that they gradually stifled patriotism and detached men from the city, wherefore the independence of the city had become less precious than the triumph of the party. This state of mind led to a new system of relations between cities.

During Polybius' time, the distinction between the two races in Greece had ceased, and the names of Dorians and Ionians were forgotten. Polybius never uses these words; it seems that he is unaware of them. The hatred against powerful cities was also appeased, and the reason for this was that there were hardly any powerful cities left; the past centuries had brought down everything that exceeded the common level. The envy of the Greeks and the cunning of foreigners had succeeded in crushing Athens; Thebes was despised; Sparta was feared at most by the Peloponnesians, for it had lost much of its prestige and strength since the various civil wars engulfed it among the other Greek cities. Hatred had naturally diminished with fear; sometimes even Sparta and Messene were seen united.

There remained only one cause of war: political factions – and they had the power to sustain what the antipathy of races, fear, and jealousy had initially brought forth. It was the quarrels of the parties that gave rise, during Polybius' time, to the quarrels between cities. The factions, from one city to another, regarded themselves as interconnected. The defeated party in one city sought refuge and assistance in the neighbouring city, which was often willing to work towards its reinstatement. Hence, there was fear, animosity, and perpetual grudges. When we see two cities fighting, it is almost always because one is governed democratically while the other is led by an aristocracy.

The same was true for alliances. When two cities were at war, each sought an ally first. They easily found a city that had the same interests and passions as itself, which is to say, where the same party dominated. It was a bond. Thus, when Mantinea had to fight against Megalopolis, it allied with Sparta; in turn, Megalopolis allied with Messene. As alliances spread in this way, Greece ended up becoming divided into two leagues.

These new confederations bore no resemblance to the one that had emerged from the common threat of the Persian Wars. It was essentially the same faction, disregarding the individual cities, that formed a confederation across several cities. At this time, however, since there were two factions in Greece, two leagues were possible, while one was not.

The Ætolians rose to power with such rapidity that their origins remain unknown, and it is unclear how exactly they grew in influence. Even before the rise of Macedonian power, Greece already feared the prospect of having to obey them.[1] Later, they alone stood against Antipater and dared to resist Brennus and the Gauls. Even before Aratus had liberated Sicyon, their league already encompassed almost the entirety of northern Greece, two-fifths of the Peloponnese, cities in Thrace, Lysimachia, Chalcedon, and even in Asia.[2] They had managed to ally themselves with nearly all of their neighbouring states except for their closest neighbours, the Acarnanians, as well as the Achæans across from them.

It is always significant for a nation to subjugate other peoples, to extend its power or influence far beyond its borders, and to share its destiny with a large number of individuals and cities. This almost justifies

---

1. Polybius, XI, 34
2. ibid, IV, 3; V, 9; XV, 23; XVIII, 21; Livy, XXXII, 33

the Ætolians in the face of insults hurled at them by the Achæan Polybius, which Livy repeats. If their virtues were only greed, avarice, contempt for the gods and oaths,[1] one could assume that they would never have risen to prominence in Greece. They would not have found so many allies if they had nothing more than the Greek language and outward appearance as assets.[2] Underneath the repugnant traits that their enemies painted, one recognises a people that is more energetic and less enervated than the rest of the Greeks. As soldiers, they were unquestionably the foremost in the Hellenic world; they may have been so in politics as well, for they were the only ones who comprehended Rome's intentions for a long time and knew how to confront her with both courage and cunning. Polybius claims that Flamininus despised their greed, but in truth he despised their power.

It seems evident that the Ætolians could not have established their empire solely through force of arms. If they dominated in such a large number of cities, it was because they had support from a party in each of them. This party was the popular party. Polybius carefully avoids emphasising this point. He is more interested in portraying the Ætolians as odious to future generations than in revealing the causes of their rise. He much prefers to depict them as avaricious individuals who seize cities in defiance of treaties

---

1. Polybius, II, 3, 45; IX, 38   2. Livy, XXXIV, 24

rather than telling us that they were called upon and supported by a party within those very cities. Only once does he indicate the close relationship between the popular party in each city and the Ætolian League when he shows us the city of Cius in Bithynia, which was both subject to all the abuses of democracy and governed by the Ætolians.[1] The same political strategy of this people is revealed by what happened in Opus in 197 B.C. – the democracy called upon the Ætolians, while the faction of the wealthy expelled them.[2] The same was true in Sparta, where the same party that overthrew Antigonus' aristocratic institutions and wanted to recall Cleomenes began by strengthening itself by bringing the Ætolians into the city.[3] The spirit of democracy reigned strongly among these mountain dwellers; aristocracy either did not exist or dared not raise its head. This popular government was strong or bold enough to decree the abolition of debts in Ætolia[4] and offer hope for it everywhere.

While the Ætolians found supporters in each city, they also had enemies in each one, which gave rise to another league. The first Achæan cities to form a confederation did so out of animus towards the Ætolians and to resist their plundering. It was originally a defensive league. At that time, almost all the cities in the Peloponnese were under the control of democratic tyrants. The oppressed aristocracy turned

---

1. Polybius, XV, 21-23   2. Livy, XXXII, 32   3. Polybius, IV, 15, 25
4. ibid, III, 1

their eyes towards this small free confederation that was emerging. Aratus liberated Sicyon and, to protect it from tyrants, joined it to the league. The king of Macedonia, Demetrius, supported the party of tyranny in the Peloponnese;[1] Aratus therefore fought against the Macedonians and captured Corinth and Megara from them. Then, when Demetrius died, leaving a son of minor age, Macedonia inspired less terror in the aristocracy and less confidence in the tyrants. Several of them voluntarily relinquished power, and Argos, Hermione, and Phlius were thus included in the league. Cleomenes, however, the leader of the democrats, held firm in Sparta. As a result, there were two opposing powers in the Peloponnese, representing the two parties.

It is evident from all that transpired that the main goal of the Achæan League was to support the aristocracy. The league relentlessly pursued tyrants and democracy, never making peace or truce with Cleomenes, Machanidas, Nabis, or the Ætolians. If it sought expansion, it was to bring the political regime enjoyed in Achæa to other cities. With each new member, the league imposed its institutions and internal laws. For instance, when Mantinea was captured, Aratus spared the lives and property of its citizens on the condition that they adopt the Achæans' system of government. Polybius acknowledges that

---

1. Polybius, II, 44

the confederation worked to extend the form of government that was in effect in Achæa and often employed force to do so.[1] Sparta, itself forcefully integrated into the league, was made to obey not only the decrees that the league could pass regarding the common interests of all its members, but also the magistrates to whom it entrusted the governance of Sparta.[2]

These confederations differ greatly from those of the preceding centuries. When, after the Battle of Mycale, all of Ionian Greece formed a league with Athens, the love for municipal freedom seemed to inspire all the confederates. Athens did not initially seek to command, nor did its allies intend to obey. Each contributed a contingent of ships or subsidies, and each sent its delegates to the common assembly. The management of the treasury was entrusted to the commissioners designated by the cities. As an additional precaution, the assembly had to be held annually in a neutral territory, in the sacred city of Delos. In favour of its power and virtue, Athens was granted hegemony, meaning the privilege of appointing the general of the allied army and directing military operations. Crucially, however, the league had no rights, no jurisdiction, no surveillance over the internal affairs of the member cities, and left each city to the independence of its own government. It existed

---

1. Polybius, II, 38, 42   2. Polybius, XXIII, 12

solely to contend against external enemies; it was formed only to repel the Persians.

It was not the same in the time of Polybius. Everyone realised that governing the city had become difficult and prone to provoking revolutions all too often. Each party experienced its own weaknesses, and they understood the need to support one another. People began to see themselves not merely as part of their own city but as part of all Greece. They gathered together all of the democratic factions and all of the aristocratic factions, forming two leagues. Established in this manner – not against an external enemy but against an internal enemy; not to secure the independence of the common homeland but to consolidate a particular party – it was inevitable and natural that their actions would primarily be directed towards the internal governance of the cities.

This was also the case in the Achæan Confederation. Polybius states that the league is not only united by an offensive and defensive alliance, but that all the cities belonging to it obey a common strategos and a shared senate. The central authority not only directs matters of war and politics but also has control over justice; all the cities recognise a common tribunal. Moreover, they share the same measures, weights, currencies, and, by extension, the same laws. Joining the league means accepting its governance and institutions, and, if necessary, the league imposes its aristocratic regime by force. The cities do not have their own finances or separate armies; taxes are paid to the confederation, which maintains a permanent army. This army is employed not only against external enemies but also against cities within the league that attempt to change their government. It appears remarkable and almost monstrous to Polybius when three cities in the league, threatened by the Eleans and not assisted by Aratus, dared to defend themselves. The cities always fade into the background; they lack a distinct history because they have no independence and do not exist on their own. We only know about Mantinea, Messene, and Argos when they join or leave the league, yet as long as they remain part of it, they disappear, lost within the confederation. The unity is complete; as Polybius says, "the Achæan League is one city, lacking only confinement within a single wall".[1]

The Ætolians were even more imperious, and the cities surrendered to them with less reservation. Of the Achæan cities, it may be said that they were at least equal among themselves, whereby all participated in the general assemblies of the league. It was still a confederation among the Achæans; among the Ætolians, however, it was domination.

Democracy willingly accepts empire; it levels the classes, does not burden the people, and satisfies their

---

[1]. Polybius, II, 37

jealousy. Aristocracy, conversely, is usually more desirous of freedom; its noble instincts make it a necessity, and, as such, the federal system is the most suitable to ensure it.

The cities that called upon the Ætolians and willingly surrendered to them had no part in the direction of common affairs. Everything was debated and decided solely among the Ætolians. Furthermore, every city joining the league received a governor to administer it – and often a garrison, as well.[1]

Federal power was thus much stronger and more despotic than it had been before, and no one thought to complain about it. For people cared less about the independence of the city than about the victory of their faction. The fragmentation of past centuries no longer existed; Greece seemed like a country where there were only two cities, but two cities in a constant state of war.

---

1. Polybius, IV, 3; XV, 23; Livy, XXXII, 33

IV

THE TWO PARTIES
THE ROMAN PARTY AND
THE MACEDONIAN PARTY

In what preceded, we have seen Greece delivered into the hands of parties and civil divisions, the city forgotten, and factions uniting minds, not in order to establish the union of Greece, but to divide it into two leagues.

Now, at this same time, the union of all the peoples of the Mediterranean was being prepared, and several signs heralded this great event. Alexander's conquest had already sown the idea in people's minds; the East, Greece, Italy, and Carthage had continuous trade and even political relations; the religions of these different peoples, once diverse, had gradually begun to align and merge. Finally, Hellenic civilisation, spread across Macedonia, the East, Egypt, and increasingly so in Italy, began to give the Mediterranean world a more uniform appearance. It so happened that concurrent to this development, almost everyone outside the Greek race – those with the power to realise such ambitions, that is – aspired to universal domination. The contenders were numerous.

The kings of Macedonia believed that, in the name of Philip and Alexander, they should not give up this ambition. Philip III, whom Polybius portrays as both odious and great, aspired, like his entire lineage, to universal empire. He was careful not to share his plans with any Greek; he had chosen an Illyrian, Demetrius of Pharos, as his confidant, along with Hannibal due to his hatred for the Romans. In the year 217, the king had his eye on everything at once: he was at war with the Ætolians, who balanced his influence in Greece; he kept a close watch over Egypt, which he coveted; and he had agents in Italy, who kept him abreast of events in Rome. It was through them that he was informed, long before the news spread in Greece, of Hannibal's descent into Italy and his rapid victories. He immediately summoned Demetrius, and the two men consulted together without witnesses. "Reconcile yourself as soon as possible", said Demetrius, "with the Ætolians; arm a fleet and descend upon Italy. Greece obeys you", he added, "one league loves you, and the other fears you. The Romans' setback presents you with a favourable opportunity, and the conquest of

Italy is the first step towards domination". Based on this conversation, it is likely that the entire plan had already been settled between these two men, and that this meeting was only about the timing and method of execution. Philip believed Demetrius and, through the mediation of Aratus, whom he involved without revealing the full plan, he ended the war with the Ætolians. With Greece pacified, he constructed a fleet of a hundred ships that would carry him to Italy. His designs constantly failed, but he always resumed them. He pursued them with energy and cunning until his death, and bequeathed them to his son. It was not for independence but for empire that he fought the Romans. "The idea of conquering Italy", says Polybius, "occupied his thoughts even in his dreams".[1]

The Seleucid dynasty, ruling over the East as inheritors of the traditions of both Alexander and the Achæmenids, also laid claim to empire. If Antiochus had only wished to escape Roman domination, he would not have shown so much mistrust towards Hannibal and would have allied with Philip.

It is not certain that Carthage consciously aspired to universal domination. Being primarily a mercantile nation and conquering only for the sake of commerce, it had reasons to think twice about an excessive expansion of its empire. It can be believed that Carthage limited its ambition to the western half of the

---

1. Polybius, V, 101-8

Mediterranean. Though satisfied ambition knows no bounds. If Carthage had become the master of what it desired, it would have exerted such influence in the world that everyone would have submitted to it, much like everyone submitted to Rome. Furthermore, having reached such a degree of power, Carthage would have been compelled to continue conquering in order to sustain itself. In addition to that, democracy was beginning to rise within the city-state, more ambitious and daring than the aristocracy. Carthage was not strong enough to suppress its people or its generals. It was being drawn, perhaps unknowingly, towards empire.

Rome, on the other hand, was marching towards it. The desire to conquer seized the Roman people from their very origins and never left them. Even when they only knew their neighbours in Latium, they did not rest until they had subdued them. As soon as they became acquainted with Italy, they did not stop until they possessed it. Their eyes turned to the world; they wanted to reign over it. Later, as masters of the civilised world, they caught sight of the barbarian world and could not resist turning their weapons against it. From its cradle, Rome had, without fully realising it, the thought of universal domination. With determined will, consistency, calmness, and confidence, it strove towards that goal.

The Greek race was thus surrounded by powers that all aspired to empire. It saw domination approaching step by step and had only to wonder when and to whom it should obey. As early as 217, these words were heard in the assembly of Greeks gathered in Naupactus: "turn your eyes towards the West, the Romans and the Carthaginians are disputing there, something other than Italy – a cloud is forming on that side; see it swell; it will burst over Greece".[1] And later, in 207, the Rhodians said to the Ætolians, who had taken up arms against Philip: "you claim to be fighting for the freedom of Greece; say it better, it is for its enslavement. You are delivering it to the Romans. Just give them the time to finish their war in Italy, and you will see them rushing to conquer Greece".[2] Thus, the Greeks were well warned. Polybius remarks that as early as 216, people paid little attention to what was happening in Greece,[3] and on every page of his book, he shows us the city-states fixing their gaze upon the foreigner, from whom they expected domination.

The Greeks, however, never harboured an especially intense hatred for foreigners. It is true that they were called barbarians, but once this satisfaction was granted to national vanity, they would happily engage with them. Throughout history, factions opened Greece up to foreigners. The party of tyrants betrayed Ionia in the Battle of Lade; they led the

---

1. Polybius, V, 104   2. ibid, XI, 5   3. Polybius, V, 105

Persians to Marathon; they surrendered Eretria and nearly handed Athens over in the midst of their triumph. During the Peloponnesian War, both sides shamelessly vied for the money, fleets, and domination of the Persians. Philip bought off the aristocracy in each city, and the democracy received gold from the Great King. There were almost always as many foreigners invited as there were factions in Greece.

Polybius himself outlined the principles of this policy. He taught us how he judged foreign intervention in principle and what he understood by patriotism and treason. "I marvel", he said, "at the gross errors that are made concerning traitors. I want to say a few words on this subject, although I admit that it is difficult and delicate, and that it is not easy to determine exactly which men should be called by this name. Clearly, not all those who have established relations with kings or powers are traitors, nor are those who, conforming to circumstances, have brought their country into a new alliance; for such men have often brought great benefits to their particular homeland. One can reproach Demosthenes for attaching this dishonourable name of traitor to the most distinguished men of each Greek city, such as Cercidas, Hieronymus, Eucampidas of Arcadia, the sons of Philiades, Neon, Thrasylochus of Messene, and others. And yet, these very same men, by calling on

Philip to come to the Peloponnese, humbled Sparta and thereby allowed the Peloponnesians to breathe and regain their knowledge of liberty. In exchange for such a favour, should they have fought against Philip? Should they not have rather worked with all their might to increase his power and glory? If they had introduced foreign garrisons into their homeland, if they had overthrown the laws of their city, and done so in the interest of their personal ambition, then they could indeed be accused of treason. But if that was not their conduct, why accuse them? They merely differed in opinion from Demosthenes; they did not believe that the interest of the Athenians was the same as that of their city". Thus, according to Polybius, these men were not traitors, nor was Demosthenes a patriot; rather, Demosthenes had one opinion and they had another. The Athenians feared foreigners, while the Arcadians needed them; and it was equally permissible for both to consult their particular interests. Calling on foreigners, seeking their assistance, involving them in the quarrels of cities or factions, seemed legitimate to Polybius and the Greeks. As long as one did not go so far as to introduce foreign garrisons into the city, one was not condemnable. It is only at that point that treason begins.

The Greeks had never strongly conceived of a common homeland, and their patriotism had hardly extended beyond the city-state. As the municipal spirit weakened, all love for the homeland diminished. Parties had surpassed the city-state in order to strengthen themselves and form leagues; similarly, they went beyond the leagues to seek support from foreigners. Before being a citizen, before being Greek, one was an aristocrat or a democrat.

Everyone undoubtedly loved freedom, but at the same time, each person, in order to seek revenge against their personal enemy, would call for subjugation. As Livy remarked,[1] they would sooner ally themselves with foreigners than yield to a fellow citizen: *"externo se potius applicat, quam civi cedat"*.

After the Lamian War, for example, Antipater was leaning towards clemency. He was about to forgive Athens and leave it free when Demades came to him, pleading for him to subjugate Athens and install both a governor and a garrison within its walls.[2]

The most honourable men in Greece shaped their politics according to the interests of their factions. The king of Macedonia, Demetrius, favoured democracy, so Aratus waged war against him and took Corinth from him. At that point, he entered into an alliance, according to Polybius, or dependence, according to Plutarch, with the Egyptian kings. He received money from Ptolemy Philadelphus and was supported by Ptolemy Evergetes.[3] If he later called upon Antigonus,

---

1. Livy, XXXIV, 49   2. Pausanias, VII, 10
3. Plutarch, *Cleomenes*; Cicero, *De Officiis*, II, 23; Pausanias, II, 8

it was because the roles had been reversed between the king of Egypt and the regent of Macedonia. Ptolemy, who ultimately had no preference for either party and sought only to create difficulties for Macedonia, momentarily had more trust in democracy and Cleomenes and so declared his support for them.[1] Consequently, Antigonus had to align himself with the aristocracy. From then on, the Achæan League hastened to call upon the Macedonians and traded Corinth and Orchomenus for the downfall of Spartan democracy.

Philip remained faithful to Antigonus' views for a short time. Whether he was frightened by the power of the Achæan League or whether he recognised, based on the experience of previous centuries, that the monarchy could gain more support from the popular party, he gradually distanced himself from the aristocracy. Demetrius of Pharos also played a role in pushing him away from the aristocracy, perhaps thinking, like Hannibal, that only democracies and kings could fight against Rome. Aratus tried to balance the power of the Illyrian. One wanted Philip to be satisfied with protecting the aristocracy and respecting the independence of Greece, while the other wanted him, with the help of democracy, to overthrow the federal system, take control of Greece, and wage war against the Romans. Philip received Aratus' advice

---

1. Polybius, II, 51   2. ibid, VII, 11; Livy, XXXII, 21; Plutarch, *Aratus*

with respect but followed the counsel of Demetrius. He revealed his new policy in Messene in 214. Both factions were engaged in a struggle for power in the city, and Aratus and Philip rushed there separately. The latter arrived first, however, and ordered, or at the very least allowed, the massacre of the aristocracy.

The next day, Aratus arrived. Philip took him aside with Demetrius and led them both to the citadel of Ithome, which he had gained access to in order to perform a sacrifice. After the animal was slaughtered, he presented its entrails to his two advisors and asked if they indicated that the citadel should be kept. "If you only have the heart of a diviner", said Demetrius, "you will leave as soon as possible. But if you possess the energy of a king, you will stay. Master of Ithome and Acrocorinth, you hold the bull by its two horns". The king then sought the opinion of Aratus. The strategist hesitated for a while, astonished or perhaps thinking it unnecessary to respond. Finally, pressed to explain himself, he said, "if you can keep this citadel without violating any oaths, I advise you to do so". Philip blushed and, once again succumbing to Aratus' influence, he said, "well then, let us retrace the path by which we came".[1]

Yet this concession did not deceive Aratus, who had uncovered the king's secret that day. He sensed that he had lost his influence and would die two years

---

1. Polybius, VII, 11; Livy, XXXII, 21; Plutarch, *Aratus*

later, so despised by Philip that it was believed he had been poisoned. Freed from this man, the king pursued his new policy more boldly. In 208, we find him in Argos, seeking popularity, laying aside the royal insignia, and pretending to blend in with the people, wanting to be seen as an equal to the masses and adopt a democratic image, βουλόμενος ἴσον τοῖς πολλοῖς καὶ δημοτικὸν ὑπογράφειν.[1]

Since the Achæan League had initially supported Philip out of hatred for democracy, distrust and enmity naturally replaced that affection as soon as Philip presented himself as a democrat. From this moment on, Polybius, the interpreter of the league's sentiments, begins to detest the king of Macedonia. Previously, Philip was said to possess such virtues as gentleness of character, moderation, and activity. Now, however, he is debauched, cruel, and faithless.

The Achæan League had to conceal its resentment for several years. What else could they do? With what force could they oppose both Macedonia and the popular party? Instead, they waited for a foreign power to present itself.

As soon as Rome appeared before the Greeks, the aristocracy was in favour of it. For the same reason, the popular party increasingly aligned itself with Macedonia. Whenever in the course of this history we see a city fighting against Rome, or serving it, let us not

---

1. Polybius, X, 25; Livy, XXVII, 30-1;

say that it loves freedom or rushes into servitude; let us say that the aristocratic party is defeated or dominant.

In 198, the people of Argos handed over the city to the Macedonians. The following year, in Opus, the party of the wealthy opened its gates to Roman troops. In the same year, the aristocracy of the Achæan city of Acarnania allied itself with Rome through a decree, which was later repealed by the people who formally declared their support for Philip, and fiercely resisted the Romans.[1]

Among the Boeotians, democracy had gained the upper hand. This, at least, is what Polybius means when he speaks of magistrates who are solely occupied with winning the favour of the people through the interruption of justice, the abolition of debts, and the distribution of money.[2] The Boeotians were therefore expected to be allies of Philip; in fact, their troops fought for him at Cynoscephalæ. However, while the entire strength of the democratic party had joined him, the aristocracy handed the city over to Flamininus. All those who had fought at Cynoscephalæ were taken prisoner. The Roman general, who still lacked sufficient experience of Greece, believed he could win over the Thebans by granting them their freedom. With their return, democracy was restored to the city, and in the very first election, despite the proximity of the Roman army, Brachylles, the leader of the popular

---

1. Livy, XXXII, 25, 32; XXXIII, 16   2. Polybius, XX, 6

and Macedonian party, was appointed Boeotarch. The wealthy citizens then went to complain to Flamininus, laying before him the audacity and ingratitude of the populace, and daring to declare that unless they struck fear into them by killing Brachylles, there would be no safety for friends of the Romans. The crime was planned by Flamininus, the leaders of the Theban aristocracy, and the Ætolian strategos; it was the latter who provided the assassins, apparently because Brachylles was too popular to find any in Thebes. Brachylles perished, but the Thebans, rather than being terrified, were more incensed by this crime and avenged it by massacring 500 Romans and killing the leaders of the aristocracy. Outnumbered, without leaders or support, they were forced to submit to the Roman general, yet as soon as Antiochus appeared, they declared their support for him.[1]

Similarly, Chalcis was handed over to Antiochus by the people. Athens remained loyal to the Romans, but not without the democratic party stirring in favour of the Syrian king. In Phocæa, where the Romans had a garrison, the populace still rose up on behalf of Antiochus, while in Demetrias, which owed its freedom to the Romans, the people were nevertheless hostile towards them.[2] Later, we shall see how news of a minor victory by Perseus sparked joy among the masses in all the Greek cities. It is therefore not true,

---

1. Polybius, XVIII, 26; XX, 7; Livy, XXXIII, 1, 2, 27, 28
2. Livy, XXXV, 39, 50, 51; Polybius, XXI, 4

as Montesquieu claims based on Polybius, that Philip had become odious and detestable to all Greeks. Macedonia was not completely abandoned by everyone, nor was Greece unanimously offering itself to the Romans. Instead, each power had its supporters and enemies in each city.

If we wish to understand the consistent preference of the Greek aristocracy for Rome, we must consider that the Roman Republic, while no longer aristocratic in its institutions, still retained aristocratic traditions and customs. The people had achieved political equality in law, but it was far from a reality. The senate had gained more authority during the war with Hannibal and for eighty years it effectively ruled the city with little opposition. Moreover, the Roman public had such a spirit that if any conflict arose, it was contained within the confines of the Forum and hidden from other nations. It was not evident in the armies, and foreigners had no knowledge of it. Greece believed that the Roman government was aristocratic. "In your country", Nabis said to Flamininus, "wealth rules and everything else is subject to it".[1]

Foreign policy was entirely in the hands of the senate. It was the senate that received ambassadors, allocated provinces, granted and extended commands, determined the number of legions, and ratified the actions of generals. While the people were consulted

---

1. Livy, XXXIV, 31

on matters of peace, it was the senate that decided the terms. In all their dealings, foreigners heard only of the senate.

Finally, it was in the senate that the plan for universal conquest was conceived, and it was the aristocracy that carried out the greatest part of it. The common people neither understood this plan nor had the desire to execute it. They often opposed the senate's intentions, recoiled from so many wars, occasionally refused to enlist, and complained that the senate only undertook these conflicts in order to deprive them of peace and tranquillity.[1]

The aristocracy of the Greek cities was therefore inclined to align themselves with Rome. In turn, Roman generals were inclined to favour the aristocracy in the cities. Flamininus, in his advice to the Greeks, recommended sensible and moderate freedom, which essentially meant an oligarchic regime under the agreed-upon terms. Before leaving Greece, he had to establish a government for the Thessalians, as, according to Polybius, they did not have one. This likely means that they were democratically governed under the influence of Macedonia. Flamininus appointed a group of senators and judges from among the wealthiest citizens to lead them, and in so doing "he ensured power for that class of citizens who have the most interest in maintaining peace", as Livy states.

---

1. Livy, XXXIV, 49, 51

Thus, a natural and close alliance united the Greek aristocracy with Rome. The wisdom of the senate and the strength of the legions would have amounted to little if a significant portion of Greece had not allied itself with Rome and tied its fate to its fortune.

This was not true only of Greece. In Italy, Spain, Gaul – everywhere the aristocracy welcomed Roman domination. During the Second Punic War, if some Italian cities remained loyal to the senate, it was because they were preserved by the aristocracy. In all of them, there were two factions; in all of them, the people were for Hannibal and the elite were for Rome. Capua surrendered to the Carthaginians because democracy prevailed there.[1] In Nola, the people "who hated both their senate and the Romans" were inclined towards defection; the aristocracy prevented it by calling for Marcellus' assistance.[2] When Croton was besieged, a defector informed the Carthaginians about the positions on the walls held by the people and those defended by the wealthy.[3] This information was enough for the city to be taken without resistance.

Even in Carthage, Rome had the affection and support of an entire faction. It was not the aristocracy that had initiated the Second Punic War, but rather the party of Barca, "strong with the favour of the army and the people".[4] Hannibal, representing democracy, relied upon it in Spain and awakened it in Italy,

---

1. Livy, XXIII, 2   2. Livy, XXIV, 13   3. Livy, XXIV, 2, 3
4. Livy, XXI, 2

essentially fighting Rome with all the democracy there was in the world. Upon his return to Carthage, unable to wage war against Rome any longer, he turned his efforts against the Carthaginian aristocracy, whereby he was denounced, exiled by them, and forced to seek refuge among the kings of the East, whom he believed would be enemies of both the aristocracy and Rome.

In the Mediterranean, then, while there are almost as many states as there are cities, there are only two factions, two interests, and two affections in people's hearts. This community of shared passions, struggles, love, and hatred already forms a sort of unity in the world. The distinction between states and cities fades away; there remains only democracy and aristocracy. The world appears to be a single city, a city where two factions are locked in bitter conflict.

V

THE FRIENDS OF LIBERTY
WEAKNESS AND INCONSISTENCY

While the people, blindly and without calculation, surrendered themselves to one or the other of these two parties, caring not for independence, there were a few men in Greece, thoughtful men, men of heart and integrity, who tried to resist the current that swept so many away. These were the same individuals we saw earlier, more moderate and less dominated by the spirit of factionalism than their fellow countrymen. In their cities, they called for the union and pacification of parties; their considered and judicious theories were meant to bring peace to their homeland. As enemies of extremes, they attempted, at least to the extent that their own fears and instinctive preferences allowed in practice, to maintain a middle ground between the excesses which they condemned in equal measure.

Since the factional temper was less powerful among them than among other men, they also distinguished themselves from their fellow countrymen in that the independence of Greece was sincerely dear to them. Just as they rejected the two extreme factions, they also rejected foreigners. Between the aristocracy devoted to Rome and the democracy devoted to Philip, they formed a kind of third party which sought to preserve liberty. Philopoemen, Lycortas, and Polybius were, in turn, each leaders of this party.

As we have seen, however, these men were not entirely free from bias. They fundamentally belonged to the aristocracy and differed from it only in their disapproval of its overreach. They feared much more the triumph of the popular party and harboured a violent enmity for it. These men devoted themselves to the independence of their homeland and gave themselves entirely to this cause; there was only one sacrifice they refused to make, which was allowing democracy to rise. They detested foreigners, but even more so the people. This was their misfortune and the inevitable cause of their weakness and inconsistency. Indeed, they might have saved Greece if they had not seen a democratic party in their midst. It seems that this sight troubled, confused, and misled them; it robbed them of their strength and at times their sagacity.

Their party, moreover, was materially very weak, like all those composed only of the enlightened class of a nation, which draws no strength from the interests or passions of the majority. Its inherent honesty and patriotism created difficulties that other parties had evaded, wherefore it would have needed a considerable degree of strength. It was also highly threatened because it had to contend internally with two extreme factions and externally with two enemies.

Worse than this weakness is the fact that the party was acutely aware of it. It was timid and discouraged from its very inception, living day by day without faith in the future, as if anticipating the imminent downfall of the cherished liberty it loved. It worked only in despair. Thus, while despising foreigners, it constantly found itself compelled to rely upon them. Aratus called upon Antigonus, Philopoemen allowed the Romans to intervene, and even Lycortas, at the very moment he feared them the most, reluctantly aided them.

The lack of political foresight is striking among these men. They seemed to be unaware that in order to avoid dependence on foreigners, one should not need them in the first place. Aratus made the mistake of calling upon Antigonus to give him Corinth and Orchomenus, believing he could force Philip to be nothing more than the general of an independent

Greece. Philopoemen was purely a soldier; at the time when deliberations were being held regarding a Roman alliance, he was busy fighting as a mercenary for the Cretans. Each of these men sided time and again with the stronger party against the weaker one – Antigonus against Cleomenes; Rome against Philip.

In vain did Philip say to the Greeks, "do not ally yourselves with the barbarians; the Romans are foreigners who should not be accustomed to Greece. They have not your language, your customs, or your laws. We, on the other hand, we Macedonians, Ætolians, Achæans, we are one people; temporary disputes may divide us, but we are united by a common and eternal struggle against the barbarians".[1] In vain did a Greek say to his fellow citizens, "threatened by Carthage or Rome, we will only escape servitude if Philip, no longer needing to maintain division among us in order to reign, can consider all of Greece as his own and thereby watch over it".[2] These warnings were not heeded; the wisest men of Greece did not understand that the foreigner was less Macedonia than Rome. The aristocracy, driven by its hatred of the popular party and eager to take revenge on Philip who supported them, declared themselves in favour of the Romans.

It was not done without hesitation or shame. While the assembly was being held in Sicyon, the Roman fleet

---

1. Livy, XXXI, 29   2. Polybius, V, 104

was anchored at Cenchreæ. Rome, Attalus, the Rhodians, and the Athenians all simultaneously exerted their influence on the council's decisions. Nonetheless, the assembly responded to the speeches of all the ambassadors with a stubborn silence that lasted for two days. It is evident that a fear of the foreigner lingered and with it a reluctance to join forces with them. Strategos Ariston spoke in favour of Rome and, without addressing the substance of the matter, emphasised the dangers of waging war against the Romans, who were masters of the sea, as well as the obvious weakness of Philip, who discredited himself by merely requesting neutrality from the Achæans. After this speech, the assembly divided into two camps and came close to engaging in physical conflict. The majority even leaned towards Philip, but ultimately, violence, intrigue, and dread influenced the assembly to side with the Romans. Several cities protested against this decision, including Megalopolis, Dyme, and Argos. The first two protested because the majority of moderate minds would have preferred neutrality, while the latter protested because the democratic party held the most strength there.[1]

Philopoemen was absent, so it is uncertain what role he would have played in the league's resolutions. What is certain, however, is that Polybius approves of them. He greatly praises Strategos Ariston for leading

---

1. Livy, XXXII, 20-23; Appian, *De Bellis Macedonicis*, 5

the Confederation into this new alliance, stating, "if Ariston had not wisely shifted Achæa's allegiance from Philip to Rome, the league would have been lost. On the contrary, it owed its security and growth to his counsel".[1] Yet, when Polybius wrote these words, he could not ignore that the decision of the assembly in Sicyon had been the origin of Roman domination in Greece.

After Rome's victory at Cynoscephalæ, these men experienced a moment of unease that Polybius does not hide. The foreigners occupied Greece, and it was necessary for them to leave, but it was clear that this could only be achieved by their own volition. Rome had the freedom to subjugate Greece, and nothing could stop it except its own moderation. The Greeks were reassured by the scene at the Isthmian Games, and the party of independence could congratulate themselves for their imprudent actions going unpunished. This, however, was itself a misfortune and the origin of a dangerous illusion. They believed that Romans were of a different nature than other men, that they faced dangers and spent their money without any ulterior motive, that they could be powerful without being ambitious. They dared to hope that Rome would limit itself to a disinterested protectorate, that it would support the Greeks against Macedonia and the aristocracy against the people,

---

1. Polybius, XVII, 13, 14

without seeking to subjugate anyone. They believed that a beneficial dependence would bring calm and peace to Greece, which only an outside power could provide, without taking away its federative system and its status as a free people. Thus, with the purest love of independence, they delivered their homeland to the Romans.

It must be acknowledged that Rome's initial policies seemed to justify this hope. Roman ambition had its stages, and Rome did not conceive the idea of subjugating the Mediterranean world all at once. Victorious over Hannibal and Carthage, Rome believed it could claim first place among the cities, but it does not appear to have immediately considered enslaving them. The first generation of conquerors distinguished itself by its prudence and restraint; it did not destroy or subjugate any city, avoided the imposition of orders, and refrained from abolishing anyone's laws. It allowed Carthage, which it had the power and right to destroy, to continue to exist; it contented itself with weakening Philip and Antiochus. For a long time, and by design, it had no other instrument of domination than the party it created within each city. Its aim was to inspire a mixture of affection, respect, and fear among the peoples, establish itself as the supreme judge above them, make the Roman senate the common tribunal of nations, regulate the government of cities, and ensure the predominance of the aristocracy in all of them. This initially appeared to be Rome's sole purpose. It hoped to achieve this through a simple federation of municipalities, with Rome at the helm. Ultimately, the first generation was satisfied with hegemony, and only the second generation aspired to empire.

During this time, the aristocracy held sway in Rome, being less audacious by nature than democracy, more calculating and cautious. It hesitated in the face of conquests, as if a premonition had indicated to them that expansion would bring triumph to democracy. It feared enslaving the world and seemed to foresee, like Scipio Africanus, that conquest could be the downfall, perhaps of Rome, certainly of the aristocracy. It was Cato who called for the ruin of Carthage every day, while Scipio repeated daily in the senate, "leave Carthage standing". Ultimately, the aristocracy, with its control over Rome's foreign policy, initially sought nothing more than the weakening of democracy and monarchy everywhere in order to reign securely within Rome itself.

It was upon these clearly expressed dispositions of the senate and the generals of Rome that certain individuals, driven by their enmity for the popular party, placed their hopes. The support of Rome guaranteed them power within their city and aided them in governing. They did not consider that a protectorate quickly transforms into domination, that one is always at the mercy of the strongest, and that the strongest themselves are rarely capable of exercising restraint. Further, even if we were to assume that the protecting power is free from ambition and undue interference, the eagerness of the protected would soon transform the alliance into an empire.

Indeed, the moderate party soon found themselves surpassed. They had merely accepted the Romans, while others had called for them. Philopoemen "only complied with the desires of Rome to the extent that they were in line with the laws of Achæa and the treaty of alliance". Then came Aristenes, who "obeyed all the desires of Rome, anticipated them, and set aside the laws of his country as soon as they came into conflict with Rome's orders".[1] In the end, those who sought the independence of their homeland had to fight not only against their fellow citizens who aspired to subjugation but also against the ambition of Rome itself.

Encouraged thus by the people, the senate did not delay in deviating from its initial moderation. One can trace in this story the simultaneous progress of Rome's ambition and the servility of the conquered peoples.

In 189, the Achæan League, whom Flamininus had just forbidden to wage war against Sparta, sent two ambassadors to Rome to support its rights. The two

---

1. Polybius, XXV, 9

delegates, however, Lycortas and Diophanes, who held differing opinions in their own country, failed to reach any agreement in the presence of the senate either. Diophanes, instead of defending the acts of the league, simply stated that it belonged to the senate to settle all matters concerning Greece and that it had the authority to resolve disputes between the league and Laconia as it pleased. Despite Lycortas' protest against this unexpected doctrine and his references to treaties and proclaimed liberty, what power did this representative of independence have between Diophanes and the Roman senate? In that session, the senate learned that its ambition, which it was reluctant to let loose, did not yet proceed quickly enough according to the desire of some Greeks.

The following year, a Roman commissioner named Quintus Cæcilius was sent to the Peloponnese, not as a mediator but as a judge between Sparta and the league.[1] Aristenes was serving as strategos, and he promptly anticipated the ambassador's wishes by convening the Achæan Senate in Argos. There, Cæcilius complained about the severity with which Sparta had been treated and urged the Achæans to rectify their mistake by relinquishing their control over Sparta within the league. Aristenes, who was expected to respond, remained silent, neither approving nor disapproving of Cæcilius. Yet the

---

[1]. Polybius, XXIII, 7

former was surpassed by others. Aristenes, once a devoted supporter of the Romans, had become lukewarm compared to other individuals. Diophanes, more zealous, had already proclaimed the dependence of the Greeks in Rome. In Argos, since the strategos still had the decency to remain silent, it was Diophanes who spoke. Amplifying Cæcilius' reproaches, he vehemently attacked the conduct of the league and added new grievances to those pointed out by the Roman ambassador. Naturally, servility begets insolence, and Cæcilius, as if initially too moderate, regained the floor and spoke with insistence and anger. The party advocating for independence clearly saw that day precisely what they could expect from the Roman alliance. This time, however, they did not succumb. Philopoemen, Lycortas, and Archon courageously responded to Cæcilius, defended the acts and rights of the league, rallied the council, and had the demands of the Roman commissioner rejected. In vain he demanded the convening of the general assembly; it was denied to him based on the country's law. The Roman left without obtaining anything, defeated but convinced that even in Achæa, there existed a party of obedience.[1]

And yet what could Philopoemen himself hope for from all this vigour of resistance? When Aristenes asked him if he was capable of facing the Romans, he

---

1. Polybius, XXIII, 10; Livy, XXXIX, 33

replied that he was well aware of Rome's power and Achæan weakness. He did not expect to resist successfully; all he wanted was to not contribute to the advancement of this invasive power, to let servitude arrive but not actively seek it. "A day will come", he added, "when the Greeks will have to obey; let us at least not hasten that day".[1] Thus, these men worked without hope, comforted not even by the bliss of delusion. They fought only to preserve the semblance of freedom for a few more days, and after every effort, even after every success, they felt themselves drawn ever closer to subjugation.

Imprudent as well as weak, this party only resisted Rome in times of peace. If Rome had an enemy to deal with, it would once again become obedient and devoted. Against Philip, the Ætolians, and Antiochus, it never failed to assist Rome in achieving victory. And only after contributing to the downfall of all those who could have aided them in their resistance, after depriving themselves of support, would they attempt opposition.

They acted thus because they feared these enemies of Rome more than Rome itself; they detested them as promoters of democracy. Their fears intensified whenever any of them took up arms, and in their terror, they clung to Rome, who would then obtain everything from them. With democracy diminished,

---

1. Polybius, XXV, 9

they wished to resist Rome, but with what means? Philopoemen himself tells us: "with reasoning first, then with prayers and wailing, and by invoking the gods".[1] They only resisted when Rome did not demand something of them; to a formal order, they would yield, satisfied with not having obeyed immediately.

One day, when a Roman commissioner, Appius Claudius, harshly criticised the Achæans for their actions regarding Sparta, Lycortas addressed him with these sorrowful words: "we are not here, I see it clearly, as representatives of a free state; we are not allies speaking before their allies – we are slaves pleading their interests before their masters. Where is the equality between you and us? We, we have only as much freedom as is granted to us; you, you are the masters". He then concluded with the following cry of independence, or rather, despair: "we respect you, Romans, and if you so wish, we fear you; but we respect and fear the immortal gods even more". This speech taught Appius nothing, except perhaps that restraint and modesty were now useless to maintain. "I advise the Achæans", he replied curtly, "to comply of their own free will, while still they may, lest they be made to do so against their will and under compulsion". The assembly let out a groan and duly obeyed.[2]

---

1. Polybius, XXV, 9   2. Livy, XXXIX, 38

The party of independence had thus reached a point where it had to summon all its courage and strength to merely express regret. It would have doubtless been better if this party, wise sixteen years earlier, had not supported the Romans against Philip and had not called upon them against Nabis. The cry for freedom only arose when it was time to submit; obedience had been given when liberty was not beyond hope.

The ambition of the Romans had only grown over the sixteen years, though not by as much as certain Greeks desired. The party of obedience gained boldness and strength with each passing day. Aristenes had been surpassed by Diophanes; soon after, Diophanes was surpassed by Callicrates.

To understand this progressive shift within the Achæan aristocracy, one must consider that during this time, even in Achæa, a democratic party emerged and gained a foothold. This party, which we will see rise to prominence so vigorously thirty years later with its leaders Diæus and Critolaus, began to gain influence and prepare its forces. As the aristocracy perceived itself to be under greater threat, it became more aggressive and domineering, as is natural. The aristocracy became a faction that increasingly distanced itself from the wisdom of Philopoemen, Aratus, and Lycortas.

On the other hand, the moderate party, seeking to maintain a balanced position between the extremes, at times supported democracy. One day, Philopoemen took up arms to defend the people of Sparta against the strategos Diophanes.[1] The aristocracy sought revenge by having Philopoemen assassinated.[2] Threatened by the emerging democracy, they turned to Rome, which they had chosen as their leader. With each setback, they drew closer to the Eternal City. Rome, in accepting the hegemony of the aristocratic party, had committed to suppressing the rabble everywhere. If the people made progress, Rome was held responsible and accused of weakness.

With the trial between Achæa and Sparta still pending, the league had sent ambassadors to the Roman senate to defend its interests. Callicrates was one of them. Instead of defending his fellow citizens, he lectured the senate on its power, rights, and duties. He scolded them for their moderation, stating that the Romans did not demand enough from Greece; it was their fault if Greece did not obey them. In every city, there was a faction that did not want any law to be weighed against Rome's desires. Yet the senate did not fulfil its duty towards the people, as it did not support its supporters; it left them exposed to the hatred and contempt of their fellow citizens and allowed its adversaries to rise to the magistracy. Therefore, Rome

---
1. Plutarch, *Philopoemen*, 24
2. ibid; Polybius, XXIV; Pausanias, VIII. 5; Livy, XXXIX

should change its policy and, by a sign of its will, inspire terror in the people.[1] The senate did not conceal its satisfaction and treated Callicrates with special honour.

It must be said that Callicrates did follow his own advice. How, after all, could one resist men who ask to obey? He openly backed his supporters, undermined his enemies, and spoke with the tone of a master. He no longer feared revealing his ambitions and rejected all the caution and compromises that invariably somewhat hinder the exercise of power.

The party of independence, crushed by Rome's ambition and the hatred of its fellow citizens, seems to have entertained the idea of seeking foreign support. During the conflicts among Alexander's successors, the kings of Egypt had supported the freedom of Greek cities against Macedonia. It was thanks to them that Aratus had been able to form the Achæan League. Philopoemen, Lycortas, and Polybius, aware of their weakness and the need for foreign support, always looked to the Ptolemaic Kingdom and attempted on several occasions to revive the ancient alliance between Egypt and Achæa. This alliance must have been, or certainly had to become, a sort of conspiracy against Rome, since it was always the friends of independence who sought it, while the supporters of Rome like Aristenes, Diophanes, and Callicrates

---

1. Polybius, XXVI, 2

hindered it.[1] Yet what could the third party achieve with Egypt against two extreme parties supported by Macedonia and Rome? What support could the Ptolemies provide to the Greeks? Indeed, it was actually Egypt that needed their assistance. One day, Egypt asked the league for a thousand soldiers, implying that it was a matter of life or death for her in the pressing danger she faced.[2]

If Greece desired to escape Roman domination, its last resort lay in Macedonia. Philip, who for twenty years read his treaty with the Romans twice a day, had never given up the idea of fighting Rome, and towards the end of his reign, he was preparing for war. What stopped him was the authority that one of his sons, Demetrius, gained over the Macedonians, as he was Rome's protégé and instrument. Through him, the senate kept a close watch on and restrained Philip. The same divisions that divided the free cities also troubled the royal courts, and Rome had friends everywhere. Despite this, the national and Macedonian party pushed Perseus upon the throne and inflicted punishment upon Demetrius. Rome did not consider itself defeated; it surrounded and captured Philip in his embittered old age. It accustomed him to the idea of disinheriting his only remaining son and replacing him with a certain Antigonus, conveniently found within the royal family, so as to remove Perseus from

---

1. Polybius, XXIII, 1; XXIX, 8   2. Polybius, XXIX, 8

the throne. Philip's untimely death, however, along with the vigour of Perseus, and perhaps popular preference, thwarted the plans of the Roman party, which consoled itself by embellishing at will the drama of Demetrius' death, the father's remorse, his wretched end, and the crimes of Perseus.

The character of the new king has been described to us only by his enemies and his victors. Nevertheless, they allow us to see in him a greatness of soul befitting a king: admirable self-control, remarkable moderation, tirelessness in his efforts, the art of knowing how to wait many years before undertaking something, and far more skill and tact in his dealings with the Greeks than Philip had displayed.

One must remember that Macedonia was still a worthy adversary of Rome. Perseus possessed such wealth that, as Polybius says, he could buy all of Greece. He could call upon seasoned soldiers and the infamous phalanx, of which a consul remarked that he had encountered nothing so formidable or terrifying. Besides the phalanx, he could enlist the assistance of the Bastarnæ and Gauls, barbarian and warlike multitudes that were already eager to pour into Italy. The strength of Macedonia was evinced by the defeat of a consul near the Peneus, by three unsuccessful campaigns, by the anxiety of the Roman people and its senate, by the extraordinary measures taken in Rome at that time, and by the need felt by Æmilius Paullus to reassure the people upon his departure.[1]

Polybius unsuccessfully attempts to conceal the fact that Perseus was very close to uniting all of the East around him and gathering all their forces to turn against Rome. Seleucus asks him to accept his daughter in marriage; Prusias asks for his sister. Egypt is on the verge of being conquered by his ally, the king of Syria.[2] Cotys, who reigns over all of Thrace, is allied with Perseus. Carthage receives his ambassadors. Even Eumenes himself, who denounced Perseus to the senate at the beginning of the war, becomes suspicious in the end.

The Greeks were opening their eyes; everywhere the Macedonian party was gaining ground. Rhodes sent ambassadors to Perseus, prepared its fleet for him, and seemed poised to put its formidable naval power, acquired over two centuries, at his disposal. Later, in the presence of a Roman envoy, Rhodes dared to deliberate, and all the Roman party could do was have the prætor send six of the forty ships that had been prepared for Perseus. The following year, the Macedonian party regained the advantage, and Rhodes compromised itself with a mediation that was more embarrassing for Rome than open opposition.[3] The Boeotians had joined forces with Perseus through a treaty; in Ætolia, a sizeable party declared its support

---

1. Livy, XLIV, 21-22; Polybius, XXIX, 1   2. Livy, XXII, 12; XLIV, 19
3. Polybius, XXVI, 7; XXVI, 3, 4, 7; XXIX, 4

for him; everywhere, the news of his initial successes stirred immoderate joy.[1] In every city, Perseus could count on the democracy, to whom he promised debt relief. What is more remarkable still is that even a part of the aristocracy leaned towards him.[2] Even in Achæa, the Roman ambassadors who travelled through the cities to gauge the disposition of minds heard nothing but murmurs in the assemblies. The council of the league, targeting Eumenes in the absence of the Romans, ordered the destruction of all monuments erected in the cities in honour of the king of Pergamum. In the midst of the federal assembly, a hitherto moderate strategos, in a very skillful speech that was both flattering for Rome and highly favourable to Macedonia, dared to hint covertly that they were preparing to change sides.[3] With so many allies – Prusias, Eumenes, Seleucus, Carthage, Greece – all that was lacking was audacity.

The opportunity was perfect for Lycortas and Polybius to work towards restoring Greece's long-lost independence. Philopoemen was dead, struck down by Rome's friends. Those who remained had no more illusions; Rome was known, bitter complaints had been made about its demands, and there had been the courage to protest loudly, even though such frankness was not without peril. Now, it required less audacity to take up arms. How could they hesitate? The Greeks

---

1. Livy, XLII, 13; Polybius, XXVII, 7   2. Livy, XLII, 30, 37
3. Livy, XLI, 23-24

were divided between an aristocracy that surrendered to Rome and a democracy that, with little honesty and patriotism, rose up against it. The true friends of independence struggled to decide between these two parties, as they were otherwise powerless to save themselves through their own strength alone. Unfortunately, the opposition to democracy and neighbouring Macedonia was stronger in them than any misgivings about Rome or the love of liberty. Polybius seems to take a genuine interest in Perseus; without loving him, he appears to lament the mistakes that led to his downfall; he has a premonition that the salvation of Greece resided in him. It is evident from his account that he hesitated to take sides. Nonetheless, he did eventually declare himself for Rome – and why? Because, as he himself states, Perseus, if victorious, would have been too formidable for Greece.[1] As if a victorious Rome should not be feared! This enmity for Macedonia, inspired by the enmity for democracy, was like a frenzy that seized the Greeks.

It is true that the third party did not wish to ally itself with the violent and corrupt aristocracy that was friendly to the Romans; it preferred to stay out of the conflict. This stance, however, simply doubled the perils they faced. Their lukewarmness towards Rome compromised them just as much as open opposition

---

1. Polybius, XXVIII, 9

would have. At the beginning of the war, Roman commissioners travelled through the cities, instilling fear in the citizens, proclaiming that they knew the level of everyone's zeal, and that they would punish the indifferent just as they would punish enemies. There were even rumours that the Romans intended to accuse Lycortas, Archon, and Polybius of secretly being friends of Perseus in their hearts.

The conduct of these Roman commissioners made the members of the third party reflect and realise that it was urgent to finally make a decision. They gathered together, with Lycortas, Archon, and Polybius, along with all the leaders of this party in the cities: Arcesilas and Ariston from Megalopolis, Stratius from Tritæa, Xenon from Patras, and Apollonidas from Sicyon. They were all in agreement in their opinions, differing only in their boldness.

Apollonidas and Stratius acknowledged that it would have been imprudent to declare themselves against Rome, but they believed that if there were those who sought Rome's favour at the expense of their homeland and laws, they must fight against them and stand their ground without flinching. Lycortas, in his usual straightforward manner, painted a picture of the situation, highlighting the equal ambition of the two powers, the same imprudence in supporting either side, and an equal danger in declaring against one of them. In his confusion and despair, he concluded in favour of absolute neutrality. Archon, undoubtedly fearful of the Romans, advised surrendering to the course of circumstances and avoiding, above all, giving rise to accusations from their enemies. Recalling the fate of a certain Ætolian, Nicander, whom Rome had punished with death for his secret friendship with Perseus, he managed to persuade the majority of the assembly. He was appointed strategos, and Polybius, having likely supported his opinion, was elected as commander of the cavalry alongside him.

The first act of the new magistrates was to reinstate the honours of Eumenes, who was then favoured by the Roman senate. Then, Archon offered the Romans the support of all the forces of the league, and it was Polybius who was tasked with delivering this offer to the proconsul Quintus Marcius.

At that time, Marcius was making great efforts and facing significant dangers in attempting to breach the entrance into Macedonia. What is remarkable is that Polybius, upon finding the Roman army in a predicament, chose to delay fulfilling his mission, instead waiting to do so until the consul, having emerged from a difficult situation, appeared to be on the verge of success.[1]

Marcius did not miss the opportunity to reject what he might earlier have accepted. The third party offered

---

1. Polybius, XXVIII, 10-11; Livy, XLIV, 3-5

him an army to appease his anger, but he refused it in order to punish them. When one of his less astute lieutenants requested 5,000 auxiliary troops from the league, the proconsul forbade the sending of such aid. Polybius happened to be in the Roman camp at that time, either as a volunteer or as a representative, and so Marcius entrusted him with the arduous task of delivering this prohibition to the Achæan League. To further compromise him, Marcius took care not to provide him with a written order. When Polybius presented himself in the Achæan assembly and announced his seemingly unbelievable mission, he was demanded to show the letters from the proconsul. His enemies could pretend to believe that he was speaking without any official orders and thus acting against the interests of Rome. His obedience gave the appearance of opposition, and soon he would suffer the consequences of it.

Of course, in his actions and writings, Polybius is completely devoted to the Romans. In his actions, he fought alongside them for some time, and in his writings, he displays a bitter animus towards Perseus and his supporters. For Polybius, the friends of Rome are always the honest men, the virtuous men, οἱ ὑγιαίνοντες.[1] If someone is a friend of Perseus, it is because they are burdened with debts and expect favours from the king. Anyone who shows an interest

---

1. "The healers"

in the King of Macedonia is portrayed as reckless and covetous. Polybius dismisses as foolish the mediation attempts by the Rhodians.[1] He is cruel and skillful in depicting the petty negotiations between Eumenes and Perseus and their struggle of greed, suggesting that it only took a few talents of silver for the King of Pergamon to become the friend of the King of Macedonia.[2] He belittles both of them, erasing any traces of greatness in Perseus. He emphasises his avarice with as much satisfaction as he previously highlighted the cruelty of Philip. He has made the father odious and now seeks to make the son ridiculous. Whether his animosity is genuine or whether he merely hopes to atone for his perceived audacious and culpable hesitations is unclear.

During the three years in which the outcome of the struggle between Rome and Perseus remained uncertain, the opposing factions throughout the Greek cities looked upon each other like enemies waiting for the moment to pounce. The suppressed animosities accumulated during these three years, ready to explode on the very day when the victory of Perseus or Rome was announced, determining in turn which faction was to become the persecutor and which would be the victim. It was Æmilius Paullus who emerged victorious, and thereafter, in all the cities, the friends of Rome indulged in joy as if they had

---

1. Polybius, XXVII, 3, 4, 6, 13; XXVIII, 15; XXIX, 7   2. ibid, XXIX, 1

achieved the victory themselves. They rushed to the consul, seeking their share of the triumph, and for each of them, this share of victory meant the ruin of their enemies in their respective cities. That is what they came in droves to ask from the consul. The Ætolians, being most eager, did not even wait for a signal to begin massacring, exiling, and confiscating. Informants from other states arrived, bringing with them lists of suspects. They came from everywhere – from Acarnania, Epirus, Boeotia, Rhodes, and from the Peloponnese came Callicrates, who singled out Polybius among many others.

It is extremely difficult for a victor to withstand so many demands. Two years earlier, when the Roman commissioners had travelled through the cities, they had resisted Callicrates and all those who accused Lycortas, Archon, and Polybius. In Ætolia and Epirus, they had been asked to condemn the enemies of Rome, and they had once again refused. As victors, they could no longer restrain the Greeks. Terror soon reigned in all the cities. The massacres in Ætolia were approved by Æmilius Paullus, who only ordered investigations to ensure that none of those slaughtered were allies of the Romans. At the urging of the informants from Greece, and based on the lists provided by them, a multitude of citizens were summoned from the various cities and arrested as suspects, then taken to Rome under the pretext of being judged there. The terror even extended to the islands. In Lesbos, the city of Antissa had harboured Perseus' fleet in its port; it was ordered to be razed, and the order was so thoroughly carried out that by the time of Pliny, there was no trace of the city left. In Rhodes, the death penalty was decreed for anyone who had acted, spoken, or even thought against Rome. In Epirus, the suspects were assassinated in their homes, in public squares, in broad daylight; anyone could kill them. Lists of proscriptions were drawn up against the wealthy and even women. Æmilius Paullus allowed everything, and as the thirst for gold and blood spread among his troops, he had to grant them in turn the plunder of Epirus, the destruction of 70 cities, and the enslavement of 150,000 people.

Achæa, which had aided Rome in its victories for thirty years, was treated no differently from the defeated. It is true that no acts, public speeches, or secret correspondence with Perseus could be alleged against them. The consul had in his possession the records of the Macedonian king, and he found nothing against the Achæans.[1] The third party, moreover, dominated in Achæa, and unlike other provinces, it had not witnessed a democratic movement stirring and making efforts in favour of Perseus. Lycortas and Archon had shown obedience, and Polybius had

---

1. Polybius, XXX, 10

shown zeal. Yet Callicrates and his friends continued to accuse the consul; they vouched for the ill intentions of their fellow citizens, and they had to be believed.

Another development which may have irritated and unsettled Æmilius Paullus is that the third party had gained a high degree of influence over the years; it had driven away the friends of Rome from power, and even in recent times, when the victory at Pydna had granted authority to the Roman party everywhere else, the Achæans had not undergone any revolution. They had retained their strategos and left Callicrates so unpopular that the Romans could even pretend to fear for his safety.

Rome, moreover, feared far more this third party, which had once served it so well, than the one which declared itself resolutely opposed to the foreign interlopers. Of the three parties, Callicrates' was devoted and sold to it; the one that, weak at the time, rose up twenty years later with Diæus, might have been useful to it; it could be part of its plans to have enemies within the cities. Only the third party caused concern and potential obstruction. If it were exterminated, either the aristocracy, having become the absolute ruler, would be able to dominate democracy forever; if it were incapable of doing so, with only two parties remaining, the struggle would soon erupt and give Rome the opportunity to strike a new blow.

Two Roman commissioners were therefore sent to Achæa. Introduced into the senate of the League, they declared that several individuals had been favourable to Perseus and ordered the assembly to pronounce a death sentence against them. They refused to identify the culprits in question and would only reveal their names after obtaining their condemnation. The assembly unanimously protested that such a procedure was contrary to justice and refused to vote before knowing the names of the suspects. One of the commissioners, pushed to the limit, dared to say that all those who had been strategoi were included in his accusation, as they all had sympathetic feelings towards the Macedonians and Perseus in their hearts. It was Callicrates who had dictated those words to him. Archon then stood up, nobly indignant, and said, "I have been a strategos, and I have no faults to reproach myself with towards the Romans, no friendship for Perseus". It was indeed him who had persuaded the Confederation to declare for the Romans. "I am confident", he added, "that I can justify my intentions, whether before the assembly of the Achæans or before the senate of Rome". The Roman quickly seized the opportunity that presented itself; it was all he wanted. He decided that all the suspects would be transported to Rome to be judged. Callicrates then read his list, which contained over a thousand names, with Polybius among them. These exiles, hostages, and prisoners, who were confined in the municipalities of Etruria, were never judged in Rome.[1]

Polybius, who affects such great disdain for Perseus, nevertheless honours him by believing that his downfall ensured Rome's universal dominance.[2] He considers Greece now subdued and disregards the few efforts that followed. Thus, of the three parties that divided Greece, one surrendered to Macedonia, and the other to Rome. The men of the third party, powerless to save their independence, obtained as the fruit of their persevering efforts only to tilt the balance in favour of Rome. Their indecisive and inert resistance was ultimately useless in the cause of liberty and disastrous to themselves.

---

1. Pausanias, VII, 10   2. Polybius, III, 1, 4, 5

VI

POLYBIUS IN ROME

Imagine an inhabitant of a Greek city arriving in Rome – they are first struck by the vastness of a city that houses 300,000 citizens. They see not the brilliant architecture and charming art of Greece, but rather monuments that astonish them with their grandeur, where everything is built for durability. They hear a language that is less harmonious and less rich than their own, but more resonant and more magisterial. Instead of a chattering people strolling under the porticoes, they see men who, after their struggles in the courtroom, go to exercise under the sun in the Field of Mars and then throw themselves into the golden waters of the Tiber.

That is what strikes his initial gaze; but as he observes Rome more closely, he is even more surprised. He sees a city without factions or civil strife, a constitution that functions regularly, institutions that remain unaltered, a political science unknown in Greece, superior military art, ardent patriotism, and strong civic virtues.

He is dazzled by the spectacle of Roman power; he encounters monuments of victory, trophies, statues of conquerors, and all the lavish glory that Rome has devised to instill pride in its people and fear in foreigners. He witnesses the pomp of triumphs and the funerals that commemorate them; the still-living memory of a war unlike any other that any people have ever endured; all the nations of the known world gathering there; embassies that flock, some seeking aid, others offering submission, almost all dressed as supplicants; a king in the garb of a freedman, and the senate allowing itself to be greeted with the title of gods. It was impossible for such a spectacle not to evoke in the soul of this Greek, not just admiration that he could feel at the sight of resplendent Athens, but also a sense of the reverence and respect that he bestowed upon divinity.

This fascination must have been irresistible. For of all the Greeks who lived in Rome, whether as hostages or as ambassadors, if their stay was brief or of some duration, there was not a single one who did not become an admirer of Rome and did not serve it upon returning to their homeland. Rome was aware of this power; one of its means of gaining supporters was to attract people to visit Rome where it could showcase itself. This power of assimilation was such that the population of the city, constantly renewed since its inception, had always been driven by the same spirit. One inevitably became Roman in Rome. Thus, Polybius was conquered. He became an admirer of the people who enslaved his homeland and persecuted him personally.

Yet nothing was more capable of winning over Polybius to Rome than the spectacle of its aristocracy. He judged Rome based on his own ideas. If he preferred it above all else, it was because he found there the realisation of all his desires regarding the governance of cities. In Thebes and Athens, he observed that "the multitude holds everything in its hands". In Crete, which is persistently praised for its wisdom, "it is governed democratically". In Sparta, power is disputed between its aristocracy and its popular party, both claiming the authority of Lycurgus. Finally, in Carthage, "the people dominate in deliberations", whereas in Rome, "the authority of the senate is still intact".[1]

Not all aristocracies are favourable in Polybius' eyes, however. We have seen his principles on politics and his preference for mixed governments. Despite being strongly attached to aristocracy, he fears its abuses and believes that, for the sake of liberty and

---

1. Polybius, VII, 44, 51

peace, a combination of democracy and monarchy should temper it. This balance of powers, this union of parties working together for the effective administration of the state, he futilely wished for in Greece, but finds realised in Rome. "One cannot tell", he says, "whether the government is a monarchy, democracy, or aristocracy". Indeed, the consuls have absolute authority in the army and hold executive power in the city. The senate controls the finances, without which nothing can be done, and the judgements that bring high-ranking individuals under its jurisdiction, as well as the direction of foreign affairs that links its fortune to the destiny and glory of the homeland. The people possess the power of electing officials, putting the patricians in their dependency, the right to vote on laws, and the veto of their tribunes. The patricians have their religion and auspices, their glory and triumphs; the plebeians have their votes and their passive resistance. Polybius does not question whether in reality the powers are as precisely balanced as they are in the laws. Though what strikes him above all is that, amidst such diversity of institutions and rights, there reigns perfect order. These three powers are interconnected, they check and moderate one another; all contribute to serving the state. Each one is so reliant upon the other two, and they are so necessary to one another, that it seems discord cannot emerge among them.

Of course, these two irreconcilable factions that have never ceased to divide humanity are to be found in Rome, as everywhere else, enemies deep in their hearts and ever ready to fight one another. The people in Rome are like those in Greece: the same passions drive them, the same needs and desires uplift their souls; they have the same innate enmity for the aristocracy. They fought for three centuries to strip the patricians of their absolute power; they gradually achieved equality of rights. Yet Polybius saw them in a moment of pause, when they halted their progress and, in a way, gathered themselves between the conquest of rights and the exercise of power.

That moment was possible because the patrician class had shown remarkable wisdom. Despite being frequently defeated, they accepted the lessons of their failures. They humbled themselves, transformed, and corrected their ways in order to maintain their rule. It was no longer the rigid and tyrannical aristocracy of the Fabii, Quinctii, and Claudii, a kind of religious caste that kept the people at a distance and refused any form of communion with them. The new aristocracy, by contrast, led by the Scipios, reached out to the people, flattered them, and feigned to owe everything to them.

Rights have become equal for everyone; the only legitimate power is that of numbers. The people are not just free; they are the masters. And here's the catch: so long as the aristocracy manages to skillfully secure a power at least equal to that which it once possessed, instead of relying explicitly and solely on birthright and institutions, it will obtain it from the people themselves.

The first Africanus is the most popular man of his time; not because, like in Greece, he corrupts the people and buys their favour through meanness or generosity; the last citizen of Rome still possesses too much dignity. Scipio does better: he wins over hearts and imaginations. "He was not more admirable", says Livy, "for his true qualities than for the art he possessed in showcasing them".[1] Every time he had to make a decision, he would ascend to the Capitol and lock himself in with Jupiter. I cannot say if the old patricians greatly approved of this affectation. Regardless, Scipio wanted the people to see clearly that he conversed with the gods. He knew that the error of the majority is the greatest power that exists on Earth.

Against the popularity of Scipio, the old laws cannot hold; the customs created by the patriciate no longer have any strength. Whether Scipio obtains magistracies at a young age or, in his old age, drags the entire people with his judges and accusers to the

---

1. Livy, XXVI, 19

Capitol, these are victories he achieves in the name of the people over the old patriciate. This same Scipio, however, is the leader of the aristocracy; he is the author of the law that grants reserved seats in the theatre to senators. Yet this aristocracy barely stirs; not the slightest murmur. Cato, who defends the old customs, despite being a plebeian, rarely finds the support of the populace.

The people, satisfied that it is to them that one must turn to obtain power, forget the struggles and revolts of previous generations. What more could they demand? What right is being contested? It is acknowledged that all power resides in the people; thus flattered and courted, they believe themselves to be more powerful; they are convinced that they reign. Thanks to this misconception, they are obedient, silencing their animosity and passions, wherefore tranquillity reigns in the city.

The factions have thus been in a state of peace for nearly a century because a skillful and enlightened aristocracy has managed to gain the upper hand. By deceiving and subduing the enormous beast, they have brought about tranquillity. It is this astute elite that thinks and acts, and through the most ingenious of devices succeed in making the people believe that it is they who think and act. The two classes are united, thanks to the naive trust of one and the indulgent and disguised dominion of the other. This is precisely what Philopoemen, Lycortas, and Polybius had dreamed of for Greece

It is but a fragile edifice that rests solely upon the error of the common people, which can be shattered by a mere movement of their hand. Let a man come and tell them that it is not they who reign, that it is not they who are wealthy, that it is not they who are happy, and immediately the base inclinations of human nature will break their dam: self-interest, greed, and jealousy resume their course, and the beautiful monument is at once overturned.

Polybius clearly saw that this peaceful state of the Roman constitution was fleeting and that it would take very little to destroy it. He witnessed too many revolutions, both in his homeland and during his extensive travels, to believe that governments can be eternal. On the contrary, according to him, they have their natural and necessary variations; they have their ages, meaning their infancy, maturity, senility, or corruption. There is an order that nature itself assigns to the progress and decline of constitutions. None can escape this law, which is so fixed and absolute that revolutions can be foreseen and marked in advance. Thus, every city has had its golden age: Athens under Themistocles, Sparta before Lysander, Carthage before the wars against Rome. During Polybius' time,

Rome finds itself in the calm and peaceful maturity of its institutions. Yet Polybius warns of the changes that await it. The development of its constitution has followed the natural order; its forthcoming revolutions are inevitable and will follow the same order.[1]

According to Polybius, the sign by which one recognises the corruption of a government is when greed seizes people's souls, when the rich, desiring their wealth to give them power, "exhaust their fortunes in distributions and corruptions that teach the people to become avaricious". The people, accustomed to expecting their subsistence from another's hand, then covet the wealth that is always placed before their eyes. They soon rise up, and in their fury, they refuse to obey. The yoke is broken, and "there is nothing but confiscation and land division until, amid their frenzy, the multitude finds a master who brings them back to monarchy". Therefore, the sequence of changes in Rome is explained, and here, as in Greece, it is once again wealth and poverty that will bring about revolutions. Before Polybius, parties fought for principles, for rights, for honours; he foresees that they will soon fight for interests.

Polybius saw Rome at the most opportune time to admire it, between the tyranny of the patricians and the struggles of the Gracchi. He does not, however, have an uncritical and servile admiration for Rome.

---

1. Polybius, VI, 9, 10, 57

He knows that some Romans are avaricious and usurious, that they can be corrupt, dishonest, and even familiar with fear, sometimes refusing to enlist against a courageous enemy.[1] Human nature has the same vices and weaknesses everywhere. If Polybius judges the Romans to be better than other men, it is not because of their virtues alone, but because of their institutions. He exclaims that Rome has the most exemplary government he knows of, and that it is impossible to find a better system of institutions.[2]

As Polybius became more acquainted with this constitution and admired it more, he must have become less fearful of a domination that could potentially grant his homeland a share in it.

As much as it was this constitution that won him over to Rome, it was also, by his own attribution, the conquest of the world. When seeking to explain this great event, he does not dwell upon the secondary causes. It is not that he fails to see them as well as others have seen them after him; here and there, he notes the senate's skill in dividing its enemies, its art of gaining supporters everywhere, its ability to dissolve alliances, and its lack of scruples in its dealings with foreigners. He sees all of this, but only in passing. These are petty tricks that did not contribute significantly to Rome's achievements, and it seems that Rome could have managed without them.

---

[1]. Polybius, XVIII, 18; XXXI, 24; XXXII, 11; XXXV, 4
[2]. ibid, VI, 11, 18

Polybius explains everything through institutions: their weakness accounts for the weakness of Greece and Carthage, while their strength accounts for the strength of Rome.

"The character of the Roman constitution", he says, "allowed Rome to subjugate Italy, Sicily, Spain, and to undertake, after the defeat of Carthage, universal domination".[1] The very position he chooses in which to explain the government of Rome shows us that it is to this constitution that Rome owed its triumph over Hannibal. In the midst of recounting the Punic War, at the very moment of crisis, he interrupts and, in a way, suspends the battle so as to introduce what must determine the victory.

How, then, are we to understand that the constitution of Rome gave it an empire? It is because throughout the world and for all minds, the great question was a question of institutions. The aristocracy placed Rome at its head because Rome appeared to be the best-governed city and inspired the most confidence. Sixty years later, the Roman aristocracy, threatened in its own homeland, would not have provided enough security to foreign aristocracies for them to gather around it. Similarly, a century earlier, the old patriciate, having nothing in common with the aristocracy of Greece, would not have succeeded in establishing an alliance. Thus, this

---

1. Polybius, VI, 1

admirable constitution, which was not intended to last long, happened to emerge precisely at the requisite time to conquer the Mediterranean world.

Polybius understood very well that Rome owed its strength and even its virtues to its institutions. Thanks to the absence or calmness of factions, it was almost the only city where politics could have unity and continuity, where one could conceive and pursue a plan without an internal revolution disrupting it. It was the only city where the public danger brought together all wills and interests, and, significantly, the only city where no one sought the support of foreigners to help their party triumph.

Indeed, there are striking historical events which speak to this. The presence of Hannibal in Italy caused all divisions within Rome to cease, as the threat he posed united the Roman factions against a common enemy. On the other hand, the presence of Scipio Africanus in Carthage exacerbated divisions within that city, as his military successes and growing influence stirred rivalries and power struggles among the Carthaginian factions.

The Romans may not have been inherently better than the Greeks, but at least public life did not wholly corrupt them. Since their entire existence was not consumed by partisan struggles, it was still possible to love the city and be patriotic. The spirit of civic duty was strong in Rome; it was not weakened by factionalism or foreign alliances. The state had significant authority over individuals and commanded great respect. Obedience to the law was commonplace, and the idea of rebelling against it was unthinkable. The true quality of the Roman people lay in their discipline. Whether in times of peace or war, at the Forum or in the camps, individual wills yielded to the collective will.

The Roman citizen considered himself as belonging to the state; no one believed they had the right to go and fight abroad and shed their blood for any interest other than that of the fatherland. The Greeks, on the other hand, had come to spill their blood indiscriminately for the kings of Syria, the kings of Egypt, and for Carthage.

The Roman citizen was attached to religion, superstition, and custom so long as they were those of the homeland. What has been said about the tolerance, or rather, indifference of the Romans is not true. The Law of the Twelve Tables explicitly forbade the worship of gods other than those of the city, stating, "*separatim nemo habessit deos, neve novos neve advenas, nisi publice adscitos*".[1] The Romans shunned foreign religions until the senate recognised them. Once a cult received the sanction of the state, however, it was

---

1. "No one shall have gods of his own, whether new or foreign, unless they have been officially admitted"

revered. Thus, the city determined the beliefs of both the individual and the public as a whole.

The fidelity to national custom is one of the primary characteristics of the Roman. For a people, it is of great benefit to share in and uphold various customs, however insignificant or even flawed they may be. They strengthen the sense of nationhood, they connect descendants to ancestors, and they help to perpetuate the homeland through the generations.

Polybius does not indulge, like Livy, in extolling the frugality, poverty, and selflessness of the forebears of the Roman people. He knows well that poverty was no more esteemed in Rome than among other men, and that wealth was never despised by those who experienced it. In a monarchy, wealth already has great value because of the well-being it provides, but in an aristocracy, it is doubly precious because it grants influence and power. Polybius sees in the Roman elite a love of silver and the habit of profit-making. "One does not willingly give away anything of one's own in Rome",[1] and if Roman law allows a debt to be paid only after three years, "there is not a man, except a Scipio, who thinks of settling it a day earlier, so excessively particular are they about money, and so profitable do they consider time". What is nonetheless admirable for a naturally acquisitive people is their respect for the state's finances. All means of acquiring wealth are fair

---

1. Polybius, XXXII, 12-13

game for a Roman, save one: enriching oneself at the expense of the Republic. The Roman is more profit-minded and more avid than the Greek, but the Greek steals from the public treasury or accepts gold from foreigners; the Roman regards the money of the state as sacred. "Entrust the guardianship of the treasury to a Greek and even if you demand ten sureties, ten signatures, and twenty witnesses, you must still expect him to break his word. Among the Romans, a magistrate handles public finances, and all that is required to ensure his compliance with the strictures of duty is a simple oath."[1]

Be he a litigant, a cruel master, a pitiless creditor, or a despotic leader, the Roman is nevertheless a good citizen. His virtues and vices work almost invariably in favour of the fatherland. At times he might be unfaithful, but never against the Republic.

While the Roman may be said to have a relatively parochial sense of justice, he does possess a very strong sense of legality. Be he well acquainted with, or a stranger to, the duties of mankind which are only written in conscience, he holds a devout respect for the very letter of what the state has established. As such, it cost a Roman little to violate an oath unless that oath had been sworn to the fatherland. The man who had initially refused to enlist became a disciplined

---

1. Polybius, VI, 56

and courageous soldier as soon as he had vowed before the gods of the city to be one.

The respect for the state and the notion of the nation's greatness instilled in every citizen a strong sense of their own dignity and duty in public life. A Roman would never show any signs of servility, greed, or fear in the presence of a foreigner.

This same respect for the state instils limitless confidence in individuals. What would never be seen in Rome is discouragement. After the battle of Cannæ, when the state was short of money, private citizens dared to finance a fleet at their own expense and recorded their expenditures, confident that they would be reimbursed. This is not merely devotion but trust, which is a precious virtue among peoples. Such confidence did not stem from frivolity or presumption; it was a result of calculation. They relied on the future of the homeland, the resources of each citizen, and the harmony of all. It was known that every endeavour would be pursued to the end. Above all, there was no fear, as in other cities, that one party would destroy what another had begun. In Rome, it was certain, unlike in most Greek cities, that the enemy had no supporters within the city. Hence the audacity of the Roman people even in their defeats and the belief of other nations "that Rome is never to be feared more than when she herself fears".[1]

---

1. Polybius, III, 75

Thus, the authority of the state was still powerful in Rome, whereas in Greece and Carthage it was weakened in almost every individual by the interests and animosities of factions. In Greece, Polybius observed that all minds were solely occupied with the quarrels of factions, and he scarcely heard anything but talk of sedition, vendettas, land distributions, debt cancellations, and foreign alliances. In Rome, on the other hand, he witnessed harmony among all, the submission of each person to the orders and interests of the city, and minds solely concerned with the expansion of the Republic.

With this constitution and spirit, Rome appears to Polybius as superior to the whole world. He is not surprised, therefore, that Rome conceived and executed the design of universal conquest. He goes even further, regarding this enterprise of subjugating the world as entirely legitimate. Nowhere does he contemplate contesting Rome's right to empire. For a practical and logical mind like his, for a man whose judgements are dominated more by facts than theories and sentiments, to understand the conquest was already a significant step towards considering it just. How could he detest and oppose an ambition that has its source in such admirable laws and will undoubtedly result in the propagation of such to other peoples? If one were to ask Polybius by what right Rome conquered the world, he would undoubtedly reply that it was by the right of its good institutions.

He became so thoroughly won over by Rome, so captivated by it, that he undertook to write the history and praise of the Roman conquest. As a disciple of Philopoemen and son of Lycortas, yet seduced by the spectacle of Rome, he ultimately took it upon himself to justify and glorify the very ambition that he had almost dared to oppose in his own country.

He begins his book at the moment when Rome conceives the desire for universal conquest, that is, at the beginning of the Second Punic War, and he follows it through to the point where Rome achieves that goal, namely, the capture of Carthage and Corinth. He shows "by what means and with what wisdom she has brought the entire world under her laws". It is truly the history of Rome that he writes; it is, in a sense, from Rome's perspective that he observes what takes place in the rest of the world. Whether he speaks of Greece, Egypt, or Spain, the thought of Rome is always present, and its influence is apparent everywhere. His work could be titled *The History of the Romans*, and indeed, that is the title given to it by another ancient author.[1] He recounts the conquest as a Roman would, so faithfully, in truth, that Livy often had only to copy from him.

---

1. Pausanias, VIII, 30

His main purpose is to explain the success and grandeur of Rome to the Greeks, who do not understand the cause.[1] They admired Rome as much as Polybius did, but in a different way. Struck by this marvellous elevation, they could not explain it through human means alone, and were thus inclined to attribute it to the favour of their most powerful divinity, Fortune. It was Fortune who willed that Macedonia remained almost inactive during the war with Hannibal; that while Philip was fighting, Antiochus did not make a move; that the same Antiochus did wage war as soon as Philip was at peace; that Hannibal was not listened to; that the northern tribes did not join forces with Perseus; that Eumenes, having been on the verge of becoming his ally, became his accuser. It was she who artfully orchestrated events to deliver one nation after another to Rome. Let us not believe that this thought was inspired by denigration, nor that they sought revenge against their masters. According to the ideas of the ancients, this thought was far from being injurious; it was customary for them to prefer attributing their successes to Fortune rather than to themselves, and the title of "fortunate" was the one in which they took the most pride.

The Greeks, both amazed and frightened by what they considered to be the mark of special favour from

---

[1]. Polybius, I, 3, 63

the gods, came to confound in their minds the idea of Rome and that of divinity. If they had explained the successes of this people, they would have simply esteemed them. Believing, however, that in Rome they saw the miraculous work of Fortune, they paid it devotion. From the first Macedonian War, Chalcis associated Flamininus with its gods, and in a city of Euboea this Roman still had, three centuries later, his temple, his priests, his festivals, and his hymns.[1] In the time of Cato, Smyrna erected a temple to the city of Rome,[2] and after the war with Perseus, Rhodes placed in its main temple the colossal statue of the Roman people.[3] Rome seemed to be of a different nature than the rest of the world.

Polybius, however, as a thoughtful man and a statesman, knows that Fortune is not the only factor influencing human events.[4] He is wary of the notion that the gods govern all things in this world and are bothered to regularly act on our behalf. For him, every human event has an unneglectable explanation and cause in the soul of man. The rise or fall of a state is, in large part, attributable to its institutions. Success does not lie outside our hands. If a city has experienced setbacks, it is because its constitution was flawed. If Rome has conquered the empire, it is because it deserved to do so.

---

1. Plutarch, *Life of Flamininus*, 23   2. Tacitus, *The Annals*, IV, 56
3. Polybius, XXXI, 16   4. Polybius, VI, 56; X, 2, 9

This idea is of a selfless spirit and a great mind. There are two ways to conceive the connection and source of historical events: one can attribute them to the action of Providence, or, to the free and meritorious work of man. The latter approach to historical analysis, while not flawless, is certainly the most fruitful in providing lessons and the most useful in practice. It is through this approach that Polybius was able to make the knowledge of past times "the best education for men".[1] Thus, his main study is "to make known the consequences, circumstances, and above all, the causes of events"; his great art is to help us understand the economy of events. It seems that he has taken something of the practical spirit of the Romans from Rome. History is neither a work of art nor a work of curiosity for him. "A sensible man", he says, "does not cultivate art for art's sake, nor science for science's sake".[2] History is a work of utility; he writes for statesmen; he wants them to learn from his book that they are the masters of events, and that it is almost always within their power to bring about success or avert defeat. From each event, they must derive practical instruction. The reading of history, therefore, is to be a preparation for the art of governing.[3]

Of the various lesson that the Greeks should draw from Polybius' work, the most important is to learn how to appreciate Rome. Polybius, by justifying the

---

1. Polybius, I, 1; III, 31-32   2. ibid, III, 14   3. ibid, IX, 1

Roman conquest through the wisdom with which it was conducted, is already working to engender an admiration for Rome in the Greeks. That is not enough, however. Above all, he aims to show how Rome uses its dominion in order to teach "his contemporaries whether this empire should be shunned or desired, and posterity whether it should rejoice or complain".[1] He answers this question through the contrast of his judgements on Greece and his judgements on Rome; through the little esteem he professes for the former and the respect he has for the latter; through the spectacle he presents to us of the turmoil and vices of his compatriots; and through the pleasure he takes in showing us the undisturbed and prudent institutions of the Romans. It emerges from his presentation of events that the work of Rome is just and good, and it is to make it appreciated and admired that he has written its history. On almost every page of his book, he seems to say to the Greeks: fix your eyes on Rome; study it closely, as I have studied it myself. Do not think of your ancient history, your ancient men of renown; all of that is insignificant compared to Rome. It is Rome that should be your model and your guide; take as much of its spirit and wisdom as you can. Set aside the little illusions of independence that you still retain. In exchange for a docility that admiration will make easy, you will receive from Rome peace, good

---

1. Polybius, III, 4

laws, and the hope of seeing these struggles that have robbed your generation of happiness and even virtue cease forever.

VII

THE LAST STRUGGLE OF DEMOCRACY AGAINST ROME

Polybius did not return to Achæa until Rome was confident that he would only serve her. Furthermore, Callicrates had already passed away, and there was no one left in Greece who could oppose his return.

At the time he revisited his homeland, it can be estimated that the members of the third party no longer existed; some had been massacred during the time of Æmilius Paullus, while the stay in Rome had transformed the remainder. Thus, between the two factions that, driven by interest and factionalism, either welcomed or detested the Romans, there existed a class of individuals who, out of wisdom, desired their rule. Rome had evidently made great progress in those twenty years.

The aristocracy, restored after the Battle of Pydna and rid of its most detested enemies, ruled peacefully in the Greek cities. The proscriptions had naturally ceased with the fear of Rome and the absence of opponents.

Even in Macedonia, it was the aristocracy that had benefited from the fall of Perseus. Æmilius Paullus had not left the country without first providing it with a constitution. He had ordered the establishment of a senate in each of the four districts, which was to be in charge of administering affairs, "lest some unprincipled flatterer of the mob should turn the reasonable liberty which had been granted by Rome into a harmful license".[1]

The kings trembled; they read in the decree concerning the affairs of Macedonia the following: "whoever already possesses liberty shall retain it under the guarantee of the Roman people; those who live under kings shall owe it to these same Romans that their monarch now exercises a more just and merciful rule; and if ever those kings should wage war against Rome, know that such an issue will bring victory to the Romans and liberty to the people".[2]

Against this declaration, capable of dissolving all kingdoms, what could the sovereigns do? None of them dared to take up Perseus' legacy. Antiochus retreated before the pride of Popillius Lænas; Eumenes hastened to Rome to beg for forgiveness; Prusias declared himself a freedman of the senate;

---

1. Livy, XLV, 18, 29, 32   2. Livy, XLV, 18

even Masinissa came to complain that the senate had sent ambassadors to demand the subsidies he was supposed to collect. Democracy endured, if meekly. Since it had hitherto resisted Rome only under the orders of the kings, one could believe that it was forever diminished along with them.

Above all the aristocracies that ruled the cities, Rome stood not as a sovereign, per se, but as the leader of the aristocratic confederation. It did not possess an inch of land in the East; it had no governors there; yet nothing was done without its assent. Callicrates had declared in the assembly of the Achæans that one could neither make war nor form alliances without the approval of the Romans.

If the senate was not yet formally the master, it was already the sovereign judge. Whenever a dispute arose between Achæa and Athens, between Eumenes and Prusias, between the two Ptolemies, or between Carthage and Masinissa, the Roman senate was called upon to act as arbiter. Let us note, moreover, that if its decisions were respected, it was not because they were always seen as the voice of justice; it was well known, as Polybius said, that it did not base its judgements on equity but on the interests of the Republic.[1]

In each city, the aristocracy held sway, with the tribunal of Rome above all, such was the order established by the senate across the Mediterranean.

---

1. Polybius, XXXII, 2

Only the democratic agitators troubled it. They remained an enemy of Rome, and nothing had been able to win them over, the Roman confederation having been been formed expressly in opposition to them. The democratic party had not yet personally measured itself against Rome, nor had it felt defeated. It was not they, but the third party that had been swept up in the fall of Perseus; it was not they who had been proscribed. The party still had all its energy and undiminished confidence in its purpose. The disappearance of the third party, which had hitherto restrained and moderated it, made it bolder and all the more aggressive. With monarchy being diminished everywhere, democracy had no more foreign support, no leader, no unity or direction; but even that gave it credibility and a certain strength, as it could now be called the party of independence.

During the twenty years that followed the Battle of Pydna, it secretly grew in strength, until suddenly it rose up on all fronts at once. This was the last serious struggle that Rome had to endure for empire. The popular party alone took up arms, and although it rose up everywhere simultaneously, it did so without coordination; there was no unity or direction despite such efforts. Each fought for themselves, yet each carried an incredible determination into battle.

It was in Spain that this fiery war, mentioned by Polybius, first took place. Allies of Rome travelled to the city to denounce the uprising, and, speaking the same language as the Achæan Callicrates, they had demanded support from the senate against their enemies, requesting that an army and a permanent governor be sent to Spain if necessary. This protracted war, ignited by a shepherd, by a bandit, only came to an end with the capture of Numantia.

Macedonia then ignites in the name of Philip. Its people have already tired of its nominally free government; they prefer to obey a king rather than a senate. They gather around the first impostor who claims to be the son of Perseus, massacre a prætor and an army, and defend themselves with more courage, as Polybius says, than they had shown under either of their legitimate kings, Philip and Perseus.

In Carthage, Appian identifies three factions: the party of Rome, the party of Massinissa, and the party of democracy. It is likely that the first two formed a single faction or, at least, they had always been united against the third. By the year 150, the democratic party, which had gradually risen in strength, became powerful enough to drive out Massinissa's supporters from the city and appoint their leader, Hasdrubal, as commander of the Carthaginian army. Massinissa besieges the city, however, and Hasdrubal is defeated.

Fuelled by fear, the aristocratic party regains control, expels Hasdrubal and his allies from Carthage, and sends numerous embassies to Rome to plead for peace at any cost. They are more than willing to hand over Hasdrubal to the Romans.

It is quite probable that twenty years earlier Rome would have accepted these demands. She would have renewed a pact with the aristocracy, content to restore their power and weaken the opposing faction. Yet Rome's ambition had grown along with its power and the obedience of the peoples. Residing at the head of a confederation was not enough; the structure was too fragile. Democracy could prevail one day among the allies; it could even emerge in Rome itself, leading to the downfall of Roman power. Rome no longer wished to rely on the obedience or strength of its allies to maintain control over the world – it desired empire. If we may judge intentions by actions, it seems that Rome had formed the idea of allowing democracy to rise up everywhere, seizing the pretext of war and vengeance where it could, temporarily confusing all parties, in order to strike and thereby subjugate everyone.

In vain did Carthage submit to Rome's demands, providing hostages, surrendering its weapons, and finally asking to be accepted as a subject. It was not a matter of obedience, but of annihilation. Carthage had to disappear or leave its shores, its ports, and its trade.

These final orders of the Roman consul had the effect of angering the people who had thus far acquiesced, provoking a democratic uprising. The envoys returning from the Roman camp were mistreated, senators deliberating were pelted with stones, Hasdrubal was recalled, and resistance against Rome swiftly mounted. The Carthaginian democracy, which had just been disarmed, fought on for four years.[1]

The same events were repeated almost exactly in Achæa. Callicrates, leader of the aristocracy and friend of the Romans, had become intolerable to the people. Polybius recounts that one day, when he had bathed in Sicyon, no one wished to enter the bath anymore, as if they considered themselves contaminated by the water that had touched his body. It is worth noting that this insult was not inflicted by the distinguished men of the city, but by the common people, for Polybius remarks that on that day, the baths were public. Even children, he adds, would call him a traitor if they encountered Callicrates on their way back from school. During festivities, public ceremonies, from the tribune to the streets, he was pursued by murmurs and jeers.

Nevertheless, they were made to endure him until the year 150, the time of his death. Another year or two passed before people became bold enough to topple his statues. None were friends to the memory of Callicrates, while Rome and the aristocracy were too

---

1. Appin, *The Punic Wars*, 68, 92

weak in countering the emerging movement. Public sentiment, however, did not immediately reach its extreme. The overflow of democracy was momentarily delayed by the memory of that defunct third party, and the statues of Lycortas were raised once again. It seemed as if people were searching for those former defenders whom they had followed too little, those noble and thoughtful friends of independence. But alas, they were no longer to be found. Lycortas' son was in Greece at that time, yet he did not offer to save freedom, nor did he take advantage of the popular fervour, which he might have tempered and directed, to accomplish the work that had been dear to him twenty years earlier. In the intervening years, he had become Roman; freedom was less precious to him, and dependence less odious. In the absence of the third party, it was only the democratic faction that sought to struggle against Rome.

The zeal of this popular movement is clearly indicated by Polybius: "the multitude", he says, "was sick and in the throes of a fever".[1] The leaders of the state at that time were Diæus, Critolaus, and Damocritus, who had been exiled during the time of Callicrates and were brought back to their homeland by the subsequent turmoil.[2] Polybius harbours the strongest animosity for them and portrays them as he usually portrays the democrats: "they are a gathering

---

1. Polybius, XXXVIII, 2   2. ibid, XL, 4

of the worst elements from each city; they are impious and a plague upon their fellow citizens".[1]

They act as the leaders of the popular party do everywhere – they abolish debts or, at the very least, defer their payment; they emancipate and arm the slaves; they acquire dictatorial power, which the people never hesitate to entrust to their favourites. The assemblies, previously composed only of the nation's elite, are then filled with artisans and low-class individuals. It is in such an assembly that the Roman ambassadors are insulted.[2]

Diodorus speaks of the violence, confiscations, exiles, and proscriptions that filled the Greek cities at that time. The popular party, either out of precaution or vengeance, disposes of its enemies and secures its victory within the cities before confronting Rome.[3] Indeed, it is once more a struggle between factions. The war begins in Sparta, and Diæus declares that he is not at war with Sparta itself, but with all those who troubled her. When asked who these men are, he lists twenty-four names from among the aristocracy.[4]

Could Polybius ever align himself with such a faction? He was, of course, among those against whom the democratic party had risen. The independence of Greece, moreover, mattered little to him if Greece were free only to be controlled by the mob. Twenty years earlier, the fear of a democracy that did not yet

---

1. Polybius, XXXVIII, 2   2. ibid, 4   3. Diodorus, XXXII, 26
4. Pausanias, VI, 12

exist had driven him into the arms of Rome. This time, he was truly confronted with democracy and its demands.

Thus, in this war, he does not exhibit the same hesitations he showed during the war against Perseus, harshly condemning the uprising: "I am going to recount", he says, "the consummation of Greece's misfortunes. It has often experienced calamities, but never equal to those which we witnessed then. The blow that struck Carthage was less terrible. Carthage, at least, did not survive its misfortune and shame. Carthage left a small space for its justification in the eyes of posterity. Greece does not provide us with the slightest pretext to excuse its faults".[1] Elsewhere, he speaks of the madness of the Greeks, and laments this struggle as unjust and sacrilegious. Rome appears moderate to him when it sends its ambassador to detach Sparta, Corinth, Argos, Orchomenus, and Heraclea from the league, and he is astonished that the Greeks have lost enough sense "to accept with the left hand what Rome offers with the right hand". He paints Greece in the darkest colours, with people fleeing the cities and running around aimlessly out of horror for the excesses committed within their walls. Some take their own lives to escape the spectacle of so much suffering; some denounce their own parents and friends to the Romans, while others denounce

---

1. Polybius, XXXVIII, 1

themselves; men seized by delirium throw themselves into wells or off the rooftops of their houses; some cities remain deserted, and, to add to the pain, the Greeks are unable to attribute these calamities to anything other than their own folly.[1]

Such remarks are not the product of an unpatriotic soul; Polybius still loved his country and was convinced that he was serving it. He simply could not accept that democracy might bring happiness to Greece. In this struggle, he did not see freedom and subjugation in opposition, but rather democracy and aristocracy, and he did not hesitate to choose between them. He believed that he was doing a great service by not taking up arms against the party of Critolaus, by not seeking Rome's vengeance. "It was the duty of a good citizen", he says, "to serve Greece by seeking to excuse it, by veiling its faults, by working to soften the anger of the conqueror".[2] And that is precisely what Polybius did. At the very moment of the conflict, he found himself by Scipio's side as he was besieging Carthage. He fought against democracy, though not in Greece; he assisted Rome with his counsel, offering his eagerness and services in exchange for the suppression of the Greek uprising, and soon he rejoiced at its rapid downfall.

These men of democracy, it must be said, were far more determined and resilient in their will and

---

1. Polybius, XL, 3   2. ibid, XXXVIII, 1

resistance than Philopoemen and Lycortas had been. There was no hesitation or hidden agenda among them. They knew exactly what they wanted and marched resolutely towards their goal. Critolaus addressed the multitude, saying, "if you are men, you will not lack allies; if you are slaves, you will not lack masters".[1] Achæa took the offensive; it declared war on Sparta and Rome and did not hesitate to send its army towards Thessaly, which was where Metellus, the victor in Macedonia, was approaching. Against Philip and Perseus, one battle had been enough. With Critolaus defeated, Achæa found a new general and a new army. "The men", says Polybius, who tries without success to conceal this final noble impulse of Greece, "brought all their wealth to the public treasury, while the women stripped themselves of their finery". The men went to fight one last time at Leucopetra; it is said that they had brought their wives with them, no doubt so that they could bear witness to their children that Greece had not fallen without a fight.

Rome was ruthless towards the democratic factions that had risen up everywhere at the same time and in such a sudden manner. Its cruelty was proportional to the energy shown by its enemy. Macedonia was definitively reduced to a province; Carthage was razed to the ground, followed by Numantia. The Romans preferred punishments that struck the imagination:

---

1. Diodorus, XXXII, 26

Cato in Spain and Æmilius Paullus in Epirus had both ordered the destruction, one of four hundred villages and the other of seventy cities, in the same hour.

Corinth, a stronghold of democracy,[1] was destroyed, its men were slaughtered, its women were sold, and its wealth and artworks were plundered. Chalcis and Thebes, two cities where the popular party had long dominated and had always allied with Philip, Antiochus, and Perseus, suffered the same fate as Corinth. After these major punishments, individual proscriptions followed, targeting the leaders of democracy in every city.

Rome was then free to establish its empire. It began by disarming Greece: all the cities that had declared against Rome demolished their walls and surrendered their weapons. Marking its new status, Greece paid tribute and received a prætor. Achæa, being the last to resist, gave its name to the conquered province.

In each city, however, it was still the aristocracy that ruled in the name of Rome. The senate's commissioners spent ten months in Greece organising a new order, from which democracy was naturally excluded.[2] Upon their departure, they entrusted Polybius, as the man who best understood the Roman mindset, with the task of ensuring that which had been established. Polybius then travelled throughout the cities, acting as a Roman commissioner, regulating the

---

1. Polybius, XXXVIII, 3   2. Pausanias, VII, 15

details of internal administration according to the plan outlined by the victors. He focused particularly on aligning civil laws with this new administration and reforming the justice system, which had been subject to constant changes due to factional disputes over several generations. He judged disputes, pacified animosities, imparted his spirit of conciliation and compliance to all, and, above all, demonstrated through his example that one could have a sincere and selfless appreciation for Rome. By way of this example, he refused the confiscated property that he had been insultingly offered. In this manner, he accustomed his fellow citizens to the imposed government and succeeded, as he himself says, in making them fond of it.[1]

The dispute between the two parties is thus definitively settled in Greece, just as it is about to begin in Rome. The aristocratic faction has emerged victorious and no longer has any opponents. As a result, passions subside, and the aristocracy, enjoying power with security, rules with moderation. The people, having transitioned from fear to indifference, remain pacified; Greece forgets the struggles that brought such calamity upon it. Life becomes more peaceful, or more productively active. Freed from the burden of public affairs and war, individuals engage in

---

1. Polybius, XL, 10

commerce and work; some indulge in pleasures, and many dedicate themselves to intellectual pursuits.

Polybius, for his part, is finally happy. He sees Greece at the end of its troubles, almost as he had wished for since childhood: a Greece without turmoil, without parties, and without sacrilege. Under the administration of the aristocracy and the rule of Rome, he declares that Greece is rising again.[1] He offers prayers to heaven that nothing may disturb the existing order, fearing "that Fortune, jealous of such tremendous joy, might delight in overthrowing it".

---

1. Polybius, XL, 14

CONCLUSION

The purpose of this work was to investigate how Greece came to be conquered by the Romans. We are fully aware that many different causes contributed to the completion of this endeavour, though the most general cause, as we believe, can be found among the Greeks themselves. Greece was torn apart by the struggles of two factions, which ravaged and corrupted it in equal measure. These factions gave birth to two leagues, and a federative system arising from such a source could not unite the Greeks. It was at that moment that the foreigner appeared, and to him they all too willingly surrendered. Can we reasonably say that Greece measured itself against Rome? We witnessed factions fight, to be sure, but did we witness the nation fight? Upon looking deep into the spirit of the age, it seemed to us that the struggle was not between two peoples but between two parties. The aristocracy brought about Rome's empire; both of them triumphed together, just as the democratic element would likely have triumphed with Macedonia. Without disputing Rome's merit and fortune, it can be said that the state of Greece, and almost the entire world, made it necessary for there to be a Rome.

In our eyes, the character and life of Polybius made this truth even more striking. We saw in him an honest and thoughtful man who sought for the longest time to remain impartial between the two factions. It was during this period that he most overtly cherished the independence of his homeland. Once he had been defeated and persecuted by his fellow citizens, however, and once impartiality was no longer possible, he came to desire foreign domination. He gave up on independence, first out of fear of democracy and then out of admiration for Rome. Without betrayal or personal interest, he believed that Roman conquest was the only recourse and hope for his country. He joyfully witnessed its accomplishment, congratulated Greece on it, and wrote a book to glorify it.

At that time, there was a higher question to be resolved for those inhabiting the Mediterranean world than the freedom of a single people. It was a question of whether the social order created by Greek and Italian genius at its origin should endure unchanged and without progress, and whether human association would remain confined within the limits of the city-state. Would the municipal system always govern humanity? While fruitful for the initial development of minds and for instilling a fondness for liberty, it had also ingrained in people a set of civic virtues, heightened human activity, and even contributed to the advancement of literature and the arts. Yet it was seemingly no longer sufficient to meet the needs of the human spirit. The principles of exclusion and animosity towards fellow Greeks – even neighbouring city dwellers – and the narrow patriotism that gave birth to so many wars and left the land in ruins, began to repel people. Connections had become too widespread, minds understood each other too well, and philosophy and the arts had made too much progress for society to remain unchanged in form.

The municipal system perished ultimately due to an internal ailment. The inequality of wealth, exacerbated and made almost incurable by slavery, brought forth two antagonistic classes. The city-state was powerless to reconcile the poor and the wealthy, two equally necessary elements upon the accord of which any well-constituted society relies. A superior authority was needed, something resembling the modern state, to govern these two opposing groups and establish equilibrium and peace between them. Over the years and many generations, as the search for such an authority stumbled on, the cities were plagued by turmoil. The conflict between factions made city life unbearable; the drawbacks of the municipal regime became extreme. People were afflicted with a kind of moral illness, marking the crisis in which nations had to undergo transformation.

Indeed, the municipal regime, having given birth to and nourished the spirit of factionalism, soon became overshadowed in the minds and affections of men by the strength of those factions.

As a consequence, the ancient love of one's fatherland, which is to say, the love of one's city, was extinguished everywhere. People no longer identified themselves as Spartans, Athenians, or Carthaginians; freedom and subjugation became indifferent matters. The question that arose among men was which faction would prevail in the city, and whether one would follow the laws of the aristocracy or those of democracy. These same struggles that we witnessed earlier, so petty and shameful, where the only thing at stake, beyond personal grievance, was wealth, struggles that embittered private life, corrupted characters, and yielded the fatherland, these were the peculiar means through which the Hellenic peoples managed to unite. To achieve this great result, one could not rely upon the wisdom of politicians or the theories of philosophers. Something more powerful was necessary, namely the instincts, interests, and even the worst passions of humanity. These factions, tearing apart each city, created a community of affections and enmities among them all, which paved the way, inadvertently, for unity. One of the two parties, in need of a leader, bestowed authority upon Rome, an authority that would soon be transformed into domination.

It was necessary for the unity of the Mediterranean world to occur in this manner, rather than through the force of arms and politics alone. The latter were not sufficient to establish a true association among peoples. A conquest achieved by them alone, even if possible, would have only resulted in forcibly bringing foreign populations closer together, and likely for a very short time. For this domination to be lasting, and especially for it to be fruitful, for a unity of civilisation to emerge from it, a voluntary and spontaneous alliance between peoples, especially Greece and Rome, was necessary. It had to be accomplished through an almost tacit agreement among nations, through an exchange where one would contribute its arts and intellect, another its knowledge of administration and laws, a third its energy and the youthful spirit of its character. Ultimately, all had to be bound together by what is most powerful: not force, not virtue, alas, but self-interest – the interest that made each one realise that to triumph over their enemies or to put an end to the struggles, they had to unite around a leader.

Hence there arose the distinctive and entirely new character of Roman domination. Rome did not conquer through enslavement; it united the world, instead, through administration. Some proconsuls may have deluded themselves about the nature of their rights, treating peoples as vanquished subjects and pillaging the provinces. Rome, on the other hand, wiser under imperial rule, was quickly accustomed to viewing itself not as a master, per se, but as the head of a vast body encompassing all peoples.

The city-states continued to exist; autonomy was granted to them because the word still held significance, and the forms of municipal governance could not be erased so quickly. Nevertheless, people became accustomed to looking beyond their cities and directing their gaze towards Rome. They still had their municipal magistrates, but it was from Rome that the true orders and irrevocable judgements originated; life flowed from Rome. There was also still a sense of regional pride; cities were praised and adorned, yet once more, it was Rome, above all, that was admired – it was the quintessential city. Soon, people desired to become Roman citizens. The city where they were born seemed small; its interests no longer preoccupied them; the honours it bestowed no longer satisfied their ambitions. They considered themselves insignificant unless they were Roman citizens. Everyone aspired to Rome, and Rome initially welcomed the leading inhabitants of the various cities on an individual basis, gradually assimilating the entire Empire. Consequently, the cities witnessed their members steadily slipping away, one after another, until the title of Roman citizen, extended to all inhabitants of the Empire some centuries later, signalled the disappearance of the municipal system. Thus, every subject became Roman, and there remained only one city that could embrace all. Rome, in time, became the common homeland of all.

Of course, the very factional struggles that had agitated the provinces soon erupted in Rome as well, producing the same effects. The municipal spirit was lost there as it was elsewhere. The population, constantly renewed by provincials and freedmen, became a mixture; the people of Rome were an assembly of all peoples, and even the senate became filled with foreigners. People became Roman in the provinces yet ceased to be so in Rome. Hence, the loss of patriotism which comes to be lamented, a patriotism that was once simply the love of one's city. Soon, in the minds of men, the homeland became the entire world. "*Patria mea totus est mundus*", said Seneca. Thus, human association expanded, and with it the arts of

Greece were revealed to all nations, the laws of Rome spread throughout Europe, and the sentiment of a shared identity took root in the hearts of the people.

GLOSSARY

CHOREGUS (χορηγός) The leader of a chorus. In Athens, the term was also used to refer to those who defrayed the cost of a performance.

PRÆTOR A Roman magistrate, ranking below consul, whose official duties included the administration of justice and commanding of armies.

STRATEGOS (στρατηγός) The leader of an army; a commander; a general.

TRIERARCHY (τριηραρχία) The office of trierarch, the commander of a trireme (an Ancient Greek ship). Refers additionally to the Athenian system whereby triremes were built, maintained, and captained for the public service.

TRIOBOL (τριώβολον) An Ancient Greek coin made of silver which was worth three obols, or half a drachma.

OTHER TITLES FROM INVICTUS PUBLISHING

On Rome and the Gods: The Life and Works of Emperor Julian

Edward Alexander

Flavius Claudius Julianus, better known to history as "Julian the Apostate", was the last Pagan Emperor to ever rule Rome. Despite his formally Christian upbringing, the nephew of Constantine the Great was irrepressibly drawn from a young age to the gods of old. With Christianity coming to predominate among the Roman elite, and Pagan religions throughout the Empire struggling to endure in the face of restrictive laws and violent coercion, Julian sought to protect, unify, and revitalise the ailing Greco-Roman faith during his tragically brief rule.

As a keen student of philosophy, Julian wrote prodigiously on a wide range of subjects including Neo-Platonism, Greco-Roman theology, just rulership, mythology, and the religious struggle between Christianity and traditional polytheism. All fourteen of Julian's extant works and an extensive collection of letters are reproduced here with an improved translation by Edward Alexander, along with an original biography of the fourth century Emperor.

OTHER TITLES FROM INVICTUS PUBLISHING

Antigone (Sophocles)
Edward Alexander

In the aftermath of a brutal war, the city of Thebes is in chaos. When the new king, Creon, declares that the body of Antigone's traitorous brother must be left unburied to rot in the sun, she boldly defies his order – an act of rebellion which sets in motion the tragic showdown between the daughter of Oedipus and the king. Sophocles' timeless tragedy explores the conflict between individual will and the power of the state, between the gods of the hearth and the polis, between loyalty to family and to fatherland. With themes of morality, justice, and duty at its core, Antigone stands among the crowning achievements of European literature, as compelling today as in the age of Periclean Athens.

Edward Alexander's masterful verse translation is accompanied by an extensive essay detailing the themes of Antigone and its relationship to Athenian history, the Homeric epics, and Ancient Greek religion. Also included in this edition is the full play in the original Greek.

OTHER TITLES FROM INVICTUS PUBLISHING

The Samurai: History, Bushidō, and the Way of the Sword
William Ashcroft

William Ashcroft's "The Samurai" traces the long and storied history of Japan's famous warrior class, detailing the great battles, legendary figures, and key developments that shaped the samurai over the centuries, together with an exploration of bushidō – the Way of the Warrior – and the art of swordsmanship, drawing on works by Yamamoto Jōchō and Miyamoto Musashi.

Ashcroft's concise history expertly charts the emergence of the samurai during the early imperial age, their rise to national dominance, and their eventual dissolution upon the founding of the modern Japanese state. Traversing over a thousand years of history, The Samurai covers such subjects as seppuku, the daring feats of Minamoto no Yoshitsune, the last stand of Kusunoki Masashige, the tumultuous Sengoku Jidai ("Age of the Country at War"), the famed vendetta of the forty-seven rōnin, and the Satsuma Rebellion – the last samurai uprising and the last civil war in Japanese history.

www.ingramcontent.com/pod-product-compliance
Lightning Source LLC
Chambersburg PA
CBHW020341010526
44119CB00048B/551